JOHN BUNYAN (1628-1688)

It is difficult to believe that a man who received little education and spent over 12 years in jail was the author of one of the most influential books of all time.

John Bunyan's classic, THE PILGRIM'S PROGRESS has been translated into over 100 languages and read throughout the world. When you read the life of Bunyan you will be inspired by how God used the faith and dedication of one man to change the lives of people all over the world. After you read Bunyan's inspiring life story, you too will be changed!

HEROES OF THE FAITH has been designed and produced for the discerning book lover. These classics of the Christian faith have been printed and bound with beauty, readability and longevity in mind.

Greatest care has gone into the selection of these volumes, with the hope that you will not only find books that are a joy to read, but books that will stir your faith and enlighten your daily walk with the Lord.

Titles available include:

John Bunyan
Fanny Crosby
Charles G. Finney
David Livingstone
Martin Luther
Dwight L. Moody
George Müller
Mary Slessor
John Wesley
George Whitefield

JOHN BUNYAN
PILGRIM AND DREAMER

BY
WILLIAM HENRY HARDING

"Behold, this dreamer cometh."—*Gen.* xxxvii. 19

Barbour Books
Westwood, New Jersey

©1988 by Barbour and Company, Inc.

All rights reserved. No part of this publication may be reproduced or transmitted in any form or by any means without written permission of the publisher.

ISBN 1-55748-033-8

Published by: **BARBOUR AND COMPANY, INC.**
164 Mill Street
Westwood, New Jersey 07675

EVANGELICAL CHRISTIAN PUBLISHERS ASSOCIATION **ecpa** MEMBER

Printed in the United States of America

Foreword

It was to another true Pilgrim that the vision came, making possible this fresh and illuminating account of the Lord's dealings with the great Dreamer of Bedford—best known by " The Pilgrim's Progress," which, besides being an English classic of the first rank, has, more than any other book save God's own Word, been the spiritual guide and counsellor of plain people, pointing them to and encouraging them in the path which leads to the Celestial City. When Mr. Harding was called into the King's presence, and passed through the River, leaving his mortal garments behind, there were many to testify to his clear witness for the Saviour he loved.

Like Bunyan, my valued friend and fellow-worker was a simple and whole-hearted follower of Christ, accepting none of the other names by which believers call themselves or are called; but rejoicing to hold hearty fellowship with all—whatever their church denomination, or

Foreword

other description—who loved the Lord in sincerity and truth.

This posthumous book reveals Mr. Harding himself and his sympathies. Humble in a remarkable degree, he was a man of noteworthy gifts of utterance, both by voice and pen, but had no time for any effort which was not concerned with the magnifying of Christ. In moments of deep feeling his almost involuntary ejaculations were linked with the Precious Name. He would have been among the last to desire praise from men, for he did not " seek his own "; but he was worthy, and it is fitting to place on record witness to this fact.

THOMAS C. MUIR.

Contents

CHAP.		PAGE
I.	THE ELSTOW BRASIER	11
II.	THE GODLY WOMEN OF BEDFORD	34
III.	EARLY ACTIVITIES	53
IV.	THE STRUGGLE FOR LIBERTY	66
V.	BEDFORD JAIL	86
VI.	"BISHOP" BUNYAN	109
VII.	THE "DEN"; AND THE BRIDGELESS RIVER	121
VIII.	THE MAN AND HIS BOOKS	143
IX.	THE "PILGRIM'S PROGRESS"	175

| *I* | *The Elstow Brasier* |

"Behold, this dreamer cometh."—*Gen.* xxxvii. 19

THE author of the *Pilgrim's Progress* is one of those outstanding sons of men who, by reason of their powerful personality, their high qualities of human sympathy, courage, and perseverance, and their extraordinary and unexpected achievements, not only command general admiration but become the peculiar intimates of the mental "inner circle" of countless thousands, generation after generation.

John Bunyan, in his plain brown suit and neat turn-down collar, with that characteristic eye-blink and expression of intermingled kindness, shrewdness and humour, is as much one of the familiar historic figures of Britain as sightless Milton dictating *Paradise Lost*, or Johnson muttering "Too-too-too" when introduced to Arthur Lee and John Wilkes at the Dillys' dinner-table, or Walter Scott, dying at Abbotsford, bidding Lockhart read the Bible to him, to the accompanying music of the rushing Tweed.

The homespun nature of our intimacy with the honest brasier of Elstow is indeed a different thing from the regard in which we hold the memory of many others of the mighty dead. If Pitt or Wellington could appear again in Westminster Hall or upon the Horse Guards Parade, golden orators and grey marshals would gather with awe to look upon "the pilot who weathered the storm," or the dour and determined soldier who "pounded" at Waterloo; but were Bunyan to pass once more by the reedy banks of Ouse or Nen, or along the beech-lined lanes towards Olney or Cambridge, every sunburnt harvester would feel it appropriate to offer him the resting-place of a poor man's cottage and a share of a poor man's bread and cheese; every humble villager would recognise that the man of sunny expression and upward look, carrying the Best of Books in his hand, was essentially at home with the common people; and, above all, the saints of the Lord would hasten, their cheeks wet with tears of joy, to greet the pilgrim of faith.

John Bunyan was born on November 30, 1628, at a cottage close to the hamlet of Harrowden, about three-quarters of a mile from the village of Elstow, near Bedford, and in a part of Elstow which was known as Bunyan's End. The Bunyans, or Bonyons, or Buignons, had been people of some consequence, and, albeit their place was now among the humblest, their line of descent could be traced so far back as to the year of the death of Cœur-de-Lion.

The Elstow Brasier

Bunyan's paternal grandfather, despite the decay of the family, was a man of some little substance, having, as appears from his will, at least a freehold cottage to bequeath. Grandfather Bunyan had two sons: Thomas and Edward. Thomas was twice married; first, when he was only a young fellow of nineteen; four years later, the young widower wedded Margaret Bentley, and their firstborn was John the Dreamer.

Part of the little home at Harrowden consisted of a forge, at which Thomas Bunyan followed the trade of brasier, and there, doubtless, little John scanned the mending of leaking pots and kettles and pans brought by the good wives of Elstow and by farmers from far and near. The field in front of the cottage sloped down to a pleasant little stream, and formed a glorious romping-ground for the boy whenever he grew tired of watching the train of sparks from the forge, or the deft play of his father with the soldering tool. The home was a plain cottage, but it was at least a substantial dwelling: the legend of the family being caravan wanderers is destitute of foundation.

John was but a boy of fifteen when his mother died; and within only two months a stepmother had come into the home. As to his education, a book of religious verse, entitled *Scriptural Poems*, and stated on the title page to be " By John Bunyan," informs us, in the introduction, that he had attended "a grammar school." If it were so, the school would be that of the Harpur Foundation, at Bedford. Dr. John Brown, however, rejects the Poems, claiming that they give no tokens of Bunyan's pith and power, and moreover pointing out that the publisher, "J. Blare, at the Looking Glass, on London Bridge," was a piratical person who is known to have issued at least one spurious book under Bunyan's name.

The position is somewhat obscure. The book was not published until twelve years after Bunyan's death. It consists of rhymed paraphrases of portions of Scripture, including the history of Joseph, the Sermon on the Mount, and the Epistle of James. There is no touch of Bunyan's pungent style from beginning to end, although the Introduction has a characteristic touch somewhat reminiscent of his readiness of expression.

Among other biographers of Bunyan, the enthusiastic Offor does not hesitate to accept the book as genuine, and Froude considers two at least of the paraphrases to be "really beautiful idylls," adding that "if we found these poems in the collected works of a poet laureate, we should consider that a difficult task had been accomplished successfully." Venables thinks this praise much too high, and doubts whether Froude had really read the Poems at all; indeed the suspicion seems well warranted in view of the fact that Froude describes them as being in blank verse when they are really in rhyme. It is difficult to accept the Poems as genuine; yet the reference to the "grammar school" may represent a fact known to the actual writer.

In any case, young Bunyan's education was of no ambitious character. Its simplicity is suggested plainly enough in *Grace Abounding:* "Notwithstanding the meanness and inconsiderableness of my parents, it pleased God to put it into their hearts to put me to school, to learn both to read and write."

The master of the grammar school at the time when Bunyan was between nine and twelve years of age was both dilatory and cruel; so that in any case the schooling of the brasier's boy was doubtless much the same as that of the other lads, his peers in adventure, who played and wrestled and fought with him upon the village green, beside the ancient Moot House, or under the shadow of the grey bell-tower.

The standard of learning among poor villagers was not high, nor were the facilities numerous. Even so late as the earlier Victorian times the scale of weekly charges displayed outside a " dame's school," in one of the counties adjoining Bedfordshire, was : " Ready, 1d. Writy, 1d. Manners, 1d."

Although as he drew towards manhood he frequented company that by no means tended to encourage spirituality of thought, he had a strong sense of the actuality of God and of the awfulness of sinning against Him. Even as a child he trembled at the thought of a Day of Judgment. As a young man, the struggles of his soul became fierce, and at times all-absorbing.

Steeling his conscience, he would seek the society of the village rowdies; yet his heart ached when he heard a professedly religious man swearing. The Christian ideal commanded his passionate admiration, although as yet he understood it only in a vague, indefinite way. Nor could he escape the conviction that the Spirit was calling him, and a mysterious Providence, he was afterwards convinced, led him as by cloud and fire and mercifully protected him. Once, his adventures took him so far from home as "a creek of the sea." Whether this was by a boat trip to the mouth of the Ouse, or a cross-country ramble to some inlet or estuary of Suffolk or Essex, does not appear. He mentions the incident only to tell of an escape from drowning. The same thought, of protecting grace, appears in the brief record of his soldiering days; he was ordered to a place of duty as a sentinel; a comrade asked leave to take the post; Bunyan consented; the substitute was killed by a musket shot.

Bunyan himself gives no precise information as to whether the Civil War found him a Royalist or a Parliamentarian. Froude claims that, since his father's sympathies were with the king, the young brasier probably enlisted with the Cavaliers. Macaulay, contrarily,

The Elstow Brasier

holds that he fought for the Parliament, in the decisive campaign of 1645, since the sympathetic military figures of the *Pilgrim's Progress* and the *Holy War* were obviously portraits of saints who, keeping their powder dry and their Bibles in constant use, marched under Cromwell or Ireton.

Tradition has persistently associated Bunyan with the forces defending Leicester against Prince Rupert. Certainly he seems to have been a private, under Colonel Richard Cockayne, in the garrison of Newport Pagnel, a town of some importance in his native county, and a military post of the Parliament; and a contingent of Newport Pagnel men aided in the defence of Leicester. Although not a large force, this column was also sufficiently effective to undertake the important task of storming the great houses—often very strongly held—of the Royalist gentry of the district. The commander, Sir Samuel Luke, was satirised by Butler—who had at one time been employed in his family—as Hudibras; but, far from being a contemptible laggard, as the Royalist poet represented, he was an able and spirited leader. Several great mansions were reduced. It may have been to one of these small sieges that Bunyan was "called to go." The details of his military life, however, remain unknown. The *Holy War* of course, suggests familiarity with the scenes of the siege of a considerable town, and such a siege could scarcely be any

B

other than that of Leicester. But the young recruit was not to be long in the ranks; a fortnight after the capture of Leicester by Rupert, Charles suffered the crushing blow of Naseby, and fled to the west.

The following year saw Bunyan back at Elstow, on the disbanding of his troop. Within two or three years he was married. All that can be traced of his wife is that she was an orphan, of godly upbringing, and very poor. They settled down in the small four-roomed house at the northern end of the village, which is still known as "Bunyan's Cottage."

How the little dwelling came to be furnished does not appear. Bunyan says that he and his bride had "not so much household stuff as a dish or a spoon" between them. Nevertheless, the young wife took with her to her humble home, stored in her mind, the teaching of a godly father, and, further, two little books which had belonged to that worthy: *The Plain Man's Pathway to Heaven*, by Arthur Dent, a Puritan writer who was rector of Shoeburyness, 1580–1608; and *The Practice of Piety*, by Dr. Lewis Bayley, Bishop of Bangor.

Hitherto, Bunyan had not evinced any desire for religious literature. His taste was rather for stories and ballads—*Bevis of Southampton* and the like, from the exciting pack of some tavern-haunting Autolycus of the villages, or from a stall in Bedford market.

Reading the two books, and listening to his wife's reminiscences of her godly father, he found new aspirations after goodness kindled in his soul; but, not comprehending the Covenant of Faith, or understanding anything of Regeneration through the Spirit, his strivings eventuated only in a painful and superstitious observance of divers forms and ceremonies. Yet, however darkly, he was groping after the light.

His confessions regarding this period of his life, with their alternating agonies of fear and inspiration, have been considered by distinguished critics to be simply the fanatical exaggerations of a jolly mechanic who has unhappily fallen into habits, understandable and pardonable, but none the less foolish, of religious maundering and introspective self-judgment.

Such criticisms, however epigrammatically put, savour but little of spiritual sagacity; their canons of life are essentially of the earth, earthy. It is not assuming a position of scolding censorship towards serious inquiry, to argue that even the most brilliant intellectual endowments and the most profound learning are qualifications that fall suddenly short when applied to an analysis of the struggles of a soul with inbred sin and fiery temptation. The retrospect of a spiritual convert, such as Bunyan gives in *Grace Abounding*, is after all not to be surveyed with accuracy, or contemplated with sympathy, apart from the illumination of the Spirit. Paul, telling of the heavenly vision, was to Agrippa an eccentric, and to Festus a madman.

Southey, in whom it is difficult to recognise a reliable guide, since he himself betrays so much of glacial formalism, declares that Bunyan "never was a vicious man"; and this dictum Macaulay holds to be "most just," urging, respecting Bunyan's own record in *Grace Abounding*, "He owns indeed that when he was a boy he never spoke without an oath. But a single admonition cured him of this bad habit for life; and the cure must have been wrought early; for at eighteen he was in the army of the Parliament; and if he had carried the vice of profaneness into that service he would doubtless have received something more than an admonition from Serjeant Bind-their-kings-in-chains, or Captain Hew-Agag-in-pieces-before-the-Lord."

The answer to such hasty generalisations is furnished in the plain statements of Bunyan himself. The stinging rebuke which he accepted was administered, not prior to his soldiering days, but after his return, and subsequent also to his marriage. His own candid admission is that he was "standing at a neighbour's shop window, and there cursing and swearing and playing the madman, after my wonted manner." Moreover, the woman herself although "a very loose and ungodly wretch," was yet stirred to protest that his cursing and swearing, " at the most fearful rate," made her tremble. She roundly denounced him as " the ungodliest fellow for swearing that ever she heard in all her life," and declared, further, that he was " able to spoil all the youth in a whole town, if they but came into his company."

Macaulay's view, that this blasphemy was a mere fleeting folly of early youth, is indeed sufficiently met by the honest confession of Bunyan the married man : " I wished with all my heart that I might be a little child again, that my father might learn me to speak without this wicked way of swearing ; for, thought I, I am so accustomed to it that it is in vain for me to think of a reformation, for I thought it never could be . . . I knew not how to speak unless I put an oath before and another behind, to make my words have authority." And however lightly Macaulay, two centuries later, regarded Bunyan's vice, the tinker's neighbours, in their day, were—to give the tinker's own words—" amazed at this my great conversion from prodigious profaneness to something like a moral life."

Southey goes so far as to admit that Bunyan was " a blackguard " ; but Macaulay thought this " too severe," on the ground that " a man whose manners and sentiments are decidedly below those of his class deserves to be called a blackguard, but it is surely unfair to apply so strong a word of reproach to one who is only what the great mass of every community must inevitably be." On this point, the spontaneous and emphatic judgment of the "very loose and ungodly wretch" seems final, particularly as it was supported by the astonished testimony of the neighbours when the profanity suddenly ceased. The woman's reproach expressly asserted the precise characteristic which Macaulay himself defined as being the mark of "a blackguard." Clearly, she was experienced in evil; yet, Bunyan was "the worst swearer she had ever heard."

Since Paul himself, despite his concurrence in the slaughter of Stephen, and his haling of other saints to prison and death, has by no means escaped the laborious attempts of men to show that he was a little excited when he spoke of himself as "the chief of sinners," it need not surprise us if, in the chilling atmosphere of the philosopher's study, the poor brasier's confessions are considerably discounted.

The true appeal is to Bunyan's confessions. It may well be conceded that heart-repentance is accompanied by an overwhelming sense of guilt and shame before God, and of awe and love which bring a swift recognition, not merely of ill deeds done, but of the soul's being altogether sick and stricken; yet it involves no departure from truth in describing the personally-realised facts, and it could not have led Bunyan to confess himself, with circumstantial details, a vile reprobate, and chief figure in blasphemy and wildness, if vile reprobate he were none. It will not do for some magician in words to assure us that these sobs of the soul are naught, and that the swearing tinker was a very pretty fellow after all. It did not appear so in Elstow ; and it is significant that in his pen-picture of himself he adopts the Pauline phrase ; it is " Grace Abounding to the Chief of Sinners."

For a considerable time prior to his being rebuked by the woman, he had at least been a regular churchgoer, having at least some vague idea, created by his wife's two little books, of searching after a better way. At first, he looked upon religion as a matter of outward observance. " I fell in very eagerly with the religion of the times ; to wit, to go to church twice a day, and that, too, with the foremost ; and there should very devoutly both say and sing as others did, yet retaining my evil life."

The struggle towards the light was long and keen. At first his aspirations were soon quenched. But he looked with profound reverence upon all that had to do with at any rate the externals of religion. His own words are : " I adored, and that with great devotion, even all things (both the high place, priest, clerk, vestment, service and what else) belonging to the church ; counting all things holy that were therein contained, and especially the priest and clerk most happy." For the honour and esteem in which he held the clergy, he "could have lain down at their feet, and have been trampled upon by them; their name, their garb, and works did so intoxicate and bewitch me."

A sermon by the vicar, Christopher Hall—an excellent and zealous pastor and preacher—upon the evil of breaking the Lord's Day, "either with labour, sports, or otherwise," deeply impressed the newly-turned blasphemer; but later in the day he was once more active in the games on the green, despite the hot smitings of the sermon. At the same time, conviction was deepening. The Spirit strove powerfully with him.

While he was lifting his stick to strike, in a game of tip-cat, a voice from on high seemed suddenly to sound into his very soul, saying: "Wilt thou leave thy sins and go to heaven, or have thy sins and go to hell?" So vivid was the impression that he gazed upwards, and seemed to see, with the eyes of the understanding, the Saviour Himself looking down upon him, as bidding him repent and turn, lest grievous punishment should overtake him.

His companions gazed wonderingly at him, doubtless speculating as to the cause of his abrupt pause, as he stood, stick in hand, gazing upwards. Then he was suddenly smitten by the self-condemning thought that he was altogether too vile a sinner to hope for forgiveness. Although in mental agony, he went on with the game.

He now resolved to harmonise his life with the despairing thought that the only comforts that could come to him were such sorry satisfactions as he could get in the ways of sin. And since he must inevitably perish, he might as well be lost for many sins as for few. Thus he continued, with a benumbed conscience, for about a month. Then came the incident of his denunciation by the ungodly woman. Not less important than her indignant upbraidings, were the counsels of a friendly adviser, who pointed him to the Bible ; for thus it was that he began to acquire that deep knowledge of Scripture which furnished him with the chief material for his influence over men, alike as preacher and author.

At first, his interest in Scripture was confined chiefly to the historical portions. The Epistles were as yet uninteresting to him. He says, indeed : " I could not away with them, being as yet but ignorant, either of the corruptions of my nature, or of the want and worth of Jesus Christ to save me." But his oaths were now much fewer, and he strove after outward reformation. While labouring to observe the Commandments, and succeeding " pretty well sometimes," he became quite self-congratulatory, and thought —as Macaulay might easily have agreed— that he " pleased God as well as any man in England." Not yet did he realise the primary truth of Christianity. He had no idea of any inward change, not understanding what was meant by spiritual regeneration, or by redemption through the blood of the cross. His verdict upon himself is : " I knew not Christ."

Bunyan's chief trouble at this time was his indulgence in the Sunday sports. The subject was a separating one. Party feeling ran high upon the matter. Puritan opposition to the games clashed with old custom, and had been intensified by the patronage given to the sports by the Stuarts ; which patronage indeed had warmed into strong advocacy.

In mediæval times, Sunday sports were allowed after Mass ; but the reforming movement produced an antagonistic sentiment, developing along the lines of the Lollards' opposition to the stage profanities, not indeed limited to Sundays, which disgraced the churchyards, and against which Grossetête and William of Wykeham agitated in vain. The struggle between the contending parties grew keen. Not easily would the great mass of the people forsake their field sports on the breezy village greens, on a Sunday evening. When action was taken by the Puritans to enforce a stricter observance, the sports party appealed to James I, and won his support ; he thereupon drew up the Declaration which is commonly called the *Book of Sports ;* it sanctioned, for Sundays, morris-dancing, archery, and other pastimes.

The Declaration was ordered to be read

from the pulpit, in every parish, but the clergy, including the Archbishop of Canterbury, protested so energetically that James bowed to the storm, and the obnoxious instrument was withdrawn.

The next reign, however, witnessed a renewal of the trouble. New monarch and new archbishop were agreed. Not only was Charles more arbitrary and less wary than the modern Solomon ; Laud, always fiercely anti-Puritan, warmly supported the royal order that the Declaration should after all be published from the pulpits. The penalties incurred by any clergyman, for refusal, were characteristic of the times ; they were suspension from the ministry and exile.

This autocratic and ill-considered action was doubtless an important factor in causing civil turmoil, and eventually the Civil War. The horror with which the Puritans regarded the Declaration is evidenced by the Bill enacted by the Long Parliament, in 1644, the year of Marston Moor, which prohibited all Sunday sports, and ordered the *Book of Sports* to be burned in public. In the intense objection to the Declaration of Charles, that was conscientiously entertained by many godly clergymen, we have also to note, not only a love for the observance of the Lord's Day, but a lively realisation of the fact that the sports were largely associated with " Saints' Days " superstitions. To Bunyan, therefore, as he emerged into spiritual understanding, the sports came to typify the world and Vanity Fair; moreover, Giant Pope.

Some of Bunyan's biographers and critics have held that in this matter his spiritual exaltation was tinged with fanaticism, but much more was involved than wrestling or tip-cat; something of the Pilgrim idea was working in the soul. He judged it an ill course, to "walk in the counsel of the ungodly." He does not mention that any of his companions partook of his aspirations. Treading the path of obedience to the heavenly light meant saying farewell to ale-shop roisterers. The world would call him "morbid crophead," and laugh prodigiously at the sour Puritanism which could keep a blithe villager from the open-air dance and the bowls o' Sundays. Was he a better man than the sinewy sons of old England, who practised their archery after Mass, and yet showed at Crecy how to speed home the grey goose shaft?

The brasier made his choice. He danced no more. It soon appeared that he must give up bell-ringing also. Such pastimes, as Macaulay notes, would have passed for virtues with Laud. Nevertheless, the separation had to be made, if the brasier meant to be a pilgrim. A man bent on quitting the City of Destruction, and having his eye upon the little Wicket-gate, recognises a change in his tastes. His joy in the gay prattle of dancing partners, and the lurid tavern conversation of lineal descendants of Ancient Pistol and Corporal Nym, begins to wane, and soon is a thing of the dead past. The common view of the day, as to bell-ringing for pastime, is revealed in the Act of 1644, which included it in the general prohibition with wrestling, shooting, bowling, masques, wakes, and dancing. Moreover, it had been the business of the ringers to sound upon their bells the signal which called the people to the sports. The associations of such bell-ringing were distinctly non-Puritan and at the same time non-spiritual.

Elstow church is the considerable and stately remnant of the church of a Benedictine nunnery, founded twelve years after the Norman Conquest by Judith, a niece of the Conqueror. The campanile subsequently built for the bells stands close to the church and upon the fringe of the village green.

It was therefore an easy matter for Bunyan, sauntering past the Moot Hall and across the grass, if not to tug at the ropes himself, at least, "letting I dare not wait upon I would," to mingle with the ringers, as a religious onlooker. This he did. Fearing, however, lest for his evil heart he should be smitten by the sudden falling of one of the bells, he carefully stood exactly beneath a main beam, assuring himself that its strength would withstand even a crashing bell. Next, he moved back into the doorway, judging that after all the bell might fall, not perpendicularly, but at an angle, striking the wall in its descent—and in such an event it might, in rebounding, crush him to the ground and kill him. Or, yet again, the tower itself might collapse upon him ; at this thought, he fled from the place altogether.

Dancing was a pastime which exercised a still more potent sway over him. A full twelvemonth passed ere he could break the spell. Doubtless, the dashing young brasier had footed it in the dance around the stump of the old market cross on the green with excellent agility ; and the argument would almost certainly be pressed home : " Since even the Act of the Long Parliament cannot suppress honest jollity, why stand out to play the part of a kill-joy ? " Among the vivacious gossipers of the long summer evenings on the green, his " moral babble " would certainly be scorned as

> ". . . the lees
> And settlings of a melancholy blood."

Nevertheless, he was no recluse, and, if attacked on the score of being a Puritan, he could hold his own quite readily, for as he says, " I was a brisk talker on matters of religion ! " Indeed, he was of necessity communicative, a " born talker." He might no longer sound a roaring stave with the bibulous ungodly, or blaspheme the man-traps on a poaching expedition, but so golden-gifted a speaker would never fail to draw a crowd, particularly as religion was a recognised subject of debate, attractive to the multitude.

Twentieth century company, from Kensington Gore to Tilbury Dock, would rather select any other topic whatsoever. Seventeenth century company accepted it, especially of course, during the Puritan ascendancy, as an entirely natural subject of discussion or conversation. Perhaps there is no more remarkable characteristic of the Civil War than the fervour with which the regiments of the Parliament would take advantage of a halt to hear a theological argument between a couple of well-read champions, on some great point of divinity, the triumph of this or that doctrinal swordsman being celebrated with a jubilance scarcely less fervent than that with which they routed the ranks of Rupert or the " man of sin " himself.

Some of these stern warriors settled in Bedford, a stronghold of the Parliament. Moreover, this was the meridian hour of the sectaries. In that extraordinary era of new-found liberty and spiritual upheaval, the Seekers, the Waiters, and the Ranters were vigorously " testifying." It was a day of opportunity; and if the liberty and independence of judgment sometimes tended headily to effervesce, in eccentricity or even fanaticism, it was yet a day of awakening, a Day of God.

Richard Baxter, young in zeal and mature in persistence, was pouring forth from pulpit and press an astonishing and pellucid flood of Gospel truth. Indeed, many high and holy messages of witness and exhortation sounded through the land. The saints did not agree on subsidiary questions, but they were one in glorifying Immanuel the Prince; and amid their bursts of praise, whether things went well or ill with them, we catch the silver sound of Rutherford's prayers for Scotland and the children of grace; and the lofty note of George Fox, wiping the blood from his wounded face, and crying, while gazing with rapt vision to heaven: " I was commanded to turn people to that inward light, spirit, and grace, by which all might know their salvation and their way to God."

The fundamental truths of Christianity, if by no means always embraced, were therefore at least matters of familiar talk in many sections of society. Biblical phrases were heard, not only in church, but in the squire's drawing-room, the market-place, and the inn-parlour; and even when the Restoration enthroned vice and folly in Whitehall, religious questions were of necessity still a dominating subject of thought and discussion, since the horrible jails of Britain were crowded with servants of Christ, and the chief domestic concern of statesmen was the problem of bringing to pass a forced Conformity.

In such a time, such a man as Bunyan, with his strong individuality, keen power of analysing systems, and growing appreciation of doctrinal truth, might with facility engage in lively discussion, and this he did. Yet, lacking the quickening power of the Spirit, he found no real profit either in debates or observances, but only a self-gratifying means of winning applause. " I was proud of my godliness," was his subsequent confession, " and indeed I did all, either to be seen of, or to be well spoken of, by men." His peace was a false peace; but the time of anchorage in God was at hand.

II — The Godly Women of Bedford

BUSINESS affairs, and perhaps the magnetic quality which a large market town possesses for near-by villagers of scanty means and economical views, drew Bunyan pretty frequently to Bedford. Proceeding thither one day, he stopped short on the main road, a little way south of the bridge over the Ouse, and close to St. John's Church, being attracted and arrested by the conversation of a small group of three or four poor women, who, while sitting out of doors in the pleasant sunshine, were talking of the things of God.

For Bunyan, those moments of quiet listening by the wayside marked the turning point of spiritual experience. The scene is one that takes life and movement in the mind. It is one of the great tableaux of religious record, of which the splendid subject is the carnal mind arrested by divine truth. It is unforgettable; the old-fashioned highway stretching away towards the bridge; the quaint little houses, with their big cross-beams and diamond-shaped window-panes; the work-worn, bright-countenanced, homely women, talking with spiritual wisdom and insight of Christ and His Kingdom; while the ruddy young brasier, who had been as ready as any for a debate on Church Government or the Presbyterian System, or maybe on the Little Horns of Daniel or the mystic meaning of the Ashes of the Red Heifer, is suddenly stayed, as though the hand of God held him, and the Spirit bade him listen to the conversation of the Land of Beulah, which is upon the borders of heaven.

As they spoke of saving grace and the work of Christ in the soul, the "brisk talker in the matters of religion" interposed no word. He simply stood still and listened with surprise and awe, while striving, almost in vain, to grasp their meaning. "I may say," is his confession, "that I heard, but I understood not, for they were far above, out of my reach. Their talk was about a New Birth, the work of God in their hearts; also how they were convinced of their miserable state by nature. They talked how God had visited their souls with His love in the Lord Jesus, and with what words and promises they had been refreshed, comforted, and supported against the temptations of the devil. And methought they spake as if joy did make them speak; they spake with such pleasantness of Scripture language, and with such appearance of grace in all they said, that they were to me as if they had found a new world, as if they were people that dwelt alone and were not to be reckoned amongst their neighbours."

Bunyan at length passed on; but he had "stared at the Pacific." He had caught a glimpse of a sunlit ocean of divine peace and love hitherto undreamed of. Indeed, these great truths of which the women spoke; the New Birth, the righteousness which is of faith, the overcoming life, the sacred majesty and spiritual loveliness of Christ; these were the subjects which occupied his mind and lips and pen from thenceforth, even to the end.

Such treasure by the roadside! Here was the secret revealed at last. Not the performance of a round of conscript duty like some blind Samson in a mill of Philistia, but, being born of the Spirit, to possess the springing well of Divine joy in the soul, and an impelling inspiration in holy service; these were delights which awaited—whom, if not John Bunyan himself?

Not immediately did he struggle into soul-rest. Terrible temptations to utter despair were yet to be encountered; a thousand doubts and fears conquered, but with a whole-souled determination he pressed still onward. Again and again he sought the company and counsel of those godly folk who could teach him so much. Using a simple, expressive sentence which had been the cry of many an awakened soul pressing into the light, and thirsting for the company of the saints, he declared: "I could not stay away."

No longer did he regard himself with complacency as a zealous religionist; no longer was he content to adore the ground the clergyman walked upon. No more was the muckrake his favourite tool. His own forcible simile was: "My mind was now so turned that it lay like a horse-leech at the vein, crying out: Give, give; yea, it was so fixed on Eternity, and on the things of the Kingdom of Heaven (that is, so far as I knew, though as yet, God knows, I knew but little); that neither Pleasures, nor Profits, nor Persuasions, nor Threats, could loose it, or make it let go its hold." The Bible was more precious than gold to him and as he studied its language it became woven into his conversation. The thought of his unworthiness would plunge him into a gulf as of Despond; then a comforting passage of Scripture would bring hope back once more.

Southey likens these fierce fights and alternating experiences of soaring and falling to being "shaken continually by the hot and cold fits of a spiritual ague"; but the comparison figures only feebly the battles of a soul which realises the loathsomeness of man's unregenerate heart, but sees no deliverance approach. "Sin and corruption," Bunyan lamented, "would as naturally bubble out of my heart as water would bubble out of a fountain." Much more than a "spiritual ague," this was an ever-deepening sense of sin. Now and again, some wonderful thought of redeeming grace would flash upon his mind as he cried out of the depths; then he would once more be overwhelmed by a sense of appalling unworthiness and guilt. The dapper debater, the theological "brisk talker," was driven to the conclusion that his sins had slain the Son of God. How should such a man wrestle on the green, lead a rollicking chorus, or chatter frivolous gossip when taking home a mended kettle?

At the very outset of his spiritual career, the creative characteristics of his mind appeared powerfully. Instinctively, he turned all to parable and story. His experiences took panoramic shape in waking dreams, in mystic visions or brooding imaginings of what might come to him, if only he had faith to believe. A rugged vein of Dante-like force and grace and fidelity runs through the spiritual tragedy of his unvarnished narrative. In a vision of the soul, he beheld those godly ones of Bedford set upon the sunny side of a high mountain, while he himself shivered below amid frost and snow, kept back by a dividing wall. Striving in his dream to find some way to join the bright company of the saints he found at length a narrow gap through which he struggled, and after much striving he emerged into the sunlight.

Translating into plain terms the truths of the vision, he showed the mountain to be the Church of God; the sun, the "comfortable shining of His merciful face" on His people; the wall, the Word, which makes separation between Christians and the world; and the gap, Jesus Christ, the Way to God the Father; while the straitness of the passage demonstrated that any who pressed through would be in downright earnest, and moreover would find no room for carrying their sins with them.

Then, in his clear realisation of the position, another paralysing fear smote him. What if, after all, there was no place for him in the Election of grace? How if God's patience and long-suffering were exhausted?

Still, in all those weary months of zigzag he gradually approached the glorious goal. His criterion of religion was therefore no longer found in religious observance; his ideal was a definite conversion, a spiritual regeneration: "I did see such glory in a converted state, that I could not be contented without a share therein. Gold! Could it have been gotten for gold, what could I have given for it! Had I had a whole world, it had all gone ten thousand times over for this, that my soul might have been in a converted state."

Further, so eager was he in his pursuit of truth that he had small regard for empty professors. He saw them clawing the things of time, " as if they should live here always." He heard them bemoan the loss of a friend, by death, in ways that proved the resurrection to hold no reality for them. Hence, with a grim cry that was at once a censure of earthworms and a reproach of his own slowness of heart, he lamented : " Were my soul but in a good condition and were I sure of it, ah ! how rich should I esteem myself, though blessed with but bread and water. I should count those but small afflictions, and bear them as little burdens. ' A wounded spirit who can bear ? ' "

In all these days of dark cloud-streak, the little forge at Elstow was still in constant action. No tongue, however bitter, has charged him with any lack of industry. The small garden at the back of the cottage would also demand the attention of so poor a man. But these were details of his struggle in life ; the real tragedy was the wounded spirit. There was certainly in all this an element of preparation for future usefulness, for his sorrows drove him closer to the Bible, and he was thus acquiring an extraordinary knowledge of the Book. He took counsel of likely neighbours ; he listened to many sermons. The texts of preachers, and passages of his own reading, worked in his mind as he went about his daily affairs ; then as he pondered, other illuminating words of Scripture would occur to him, gilding his path with light. The text of a sermon : " Behold, thou art fair, My love " (Cant. i. 15), delighted him with thoughts of the true Church of Christ being loved by Him under all circumstances whatsoever ; and with this he linked the Pauline declaration : that " neither height, nor depth, nor any other creature, shall be able to separate us from the love of God, which is in Christ Jesus our Lord."

Almost in the tender consolation of such a melting reverie, almost he could believe that his sins would be forgiven ; indeed, so overflowingly glad was he with gratitude for Divine love and mercy, that, seeing some crows upon the ploughed land before him, he felt that had that feathered congregation been able to understand, he would have spoken even to them of the mercy and love of God to John Bunyan the brasier. The crows, however, might shortly have become disappointed with their fervent lecturer, for he was soon wandering disconsolate in a tangled forest of terrifying doubts. The words : " Satan hath desired to have you," sounded so strongly in his ears that he actually looked back down the road, half expecting to see some caller following him.

Spiritual darkness swept down upon him, like a storm on Gennesaret. A flood of blasphemous whispers, like those which he afterwards visioned as hissed by the gibbering phantoms of the Valley of the Shadow of Death, filled his revolting ears. He feared that he was devil-possessed; the Scriptures, too, gave him many a stroke—as, for example, when he read in Isa. lvii. 20, 21 : " The wicked are like the troubled sea, when it cannot rest, whose waters cast up mire and dirt. There is no peace, saith my God, to the wicked."

During the latter part of these agonising wrestlings, Bunyan was greatly helped by a book and a man. The book was Luther's *Commentary on the Epistle to the Galatians;* the man was John Gifford, pastor of the congregation of Independents, at Bedford; which congregation included the godly women of the roadside conversation and the vision of the walled mountain. Of the book—an old and worn copy, almost ready to fall to pieces at a touch—Bunyan says: " I do prefer this book of Martin Luther upon the Galatians (except the Holy Bible) before all books that ever I have seen, as most fit for a wounded conscience."

As for Gifford, he was a man of saintly life —Bunyan styles him " holy Mr. Gifford "— and large abilities, who after passing through desperate adventures and chequered experiences, had come to taste the heavenly manna, and to minister to the saints. As a major in the king's forces, he had been engaged in the severe hand-to-hand battle in the streets of Maidstone, in 1648, in which Fairfax quenched the rising of the Kentish Royalists. Though taken prisoner, and sentenced to be hanged,

Gifford managed to escape, and after being long hidden in nooks and corners, he appeared at Bedford in the guise of a physician, for which profession he had probably been educated. This change of avocation, however, still left him a drunkard and gamester, of the school of the dissolute Goring; but being suddenly smitten with a profound conviction of sin, he sought Divine mercy and believed unto salvation. The wine-bibbing warrior was changed into a godly preacher and expositor; and gathering round him a little group of converts and interested hearers, he found himself chosen by them to be their " pastor, or elder, to minister to them the things of the Kingdom of Christ."

Such a man would be peculiarly well adapted to guide and counsel a fearful and trembling seeker like Bunyan. The principles of the little church were, briefly: " Faith in Christ and Holiness of life." The thorough-going character of the teaching appears from Bunyan's hint, that Gifford "made it his business to deliver the people of God from all those false and unsound rests that, by nature, we are prone to take and make to our souls." Moreover, the studious brasier found an excellent encouragement to devote himself with fresh joy to the Bible as a treasure-store: " Oh! Now, how was my soul led from truth to truth by God! Even from the Birth and cradle of the Son of God to His

Ascension and Second Coming from Heaven to judge the world."

Even so, it was only by slow degrees that the skies cleared, and that a settled rest in God came to the weary soul of this imaginative disciple. A great deal of his trouble arose from his intense sense of unfitness. Such ingratitude as his, such a lack of living faith, such wretched changeableness, seemed to him to be beyond forgiveness. Once, the fear smote him that he had committed the unpardonable sin; and a foolish person to whom he mentioned the matter agreed that this was probably a correct view.

In another cloud of gloom, Bunyan thought himself like Peter, denying Christ; like Judas, betraying Him; or like Esau, selling his birthright. A study of the terrible end of Francis Spira aggravated his misery. He read how Spira, a successful and popular Italian lawyer, abandoned Reformation principles, when threatened by the Papal Legate at Venice; how, like Cranmer, he repented his recantation, but, swayed by the entreaties of his family he failed to make an open confession of the fact. He read, finally, how Spira, tormented by conscience and despairing of Divine forgiveness, at length refused food and died in extreme agony, his physical anguish the least of his woes. The tragic story was to Bunyan's troubled soul " as salt when rubbed into a fresh wound." The groans of the despairing Italian seemed to ring in his ears. They were, he says, "as knives and daggers to my soul; especially that sentence of his was frightful unto me: 'Man knows the beginnings of sin, but who bounds the issues thereof?'"

Yet again sweet rays of mercy flashed upon his darkened outlook, so that the dolorous record is interwoven with illustrations of penitence and pleading, from the story of Benhadad's servants, going with ropes upon their heads to beseech mercy from the King of Israel, to that of the Canaanitish woman, pleading that succour might be vouchsafed her, even as a fragment that falls to the ground from the children's table.

That some writers, among the many who have touched upon Bunyan's distresses at this period of his career, should have suggested that he was altogether beside himself, is not surprising, for his own plain word is: "I thought I should be bereft of my wits." This fear expressed, however, not the confused murmuring of a vain and self-centred fanatic, but the godly fear that the blasphemous thoughts which plagued him, unfitted him to love and serve God, and would prove a separating bar from the favour of the All-Pure and the All-Righteous.

Although he has been stigmatised as practically a self-torturer, a subject of delusions and a creator of artificial miseries, there is nothing hysterical in his story. The Confessions of Bunyan, in *Grace Abounding*, are as sane and reasonable as those of Augustine. Bunyan feared to stand inside the bell tower, lest the bells should fall and kill him and his soul be lost: Augustine could not bear to abide in the house. The poor brasier seemed to hear a voice calling to him from heaven, upon Elstow green; so did the son of Monica under the fig-tree in the garden at Milan. To seek earnestly with agonising prayers and tears and many a bitter fear, the victory that overcometh the world, may indeed be a very midsummer madness in the judgment of the majority; yet, on the other hand, there is Bunyan's view, the plain view of the Christian, that the truly wise are those who are fixedly resolved, whether struggling or trusting, whether in anguish or winning through to the rest of faith, to respond to the call which bids them not to be conformed to this world, but to be transformed by the renewing of the mind, that they may prove what is the good, and acceptable, and perfect, will of God.

Venables ascribes Bunyan's long and tragic experiences partly to his "unhappy mode of dealing with the Bible as a collection of texts." That he pondered and studied single texts is true, and he did so to his profit. For example, he found, naturally enough, a wonderful sweetness in, "I have loved thee with an everlasting love." At the same time he compared and weighed Scripture with Scripture. His first books, and the character of his early reputation, demonstrate that the knowledge he acquired of the Bible was not shallow and merely textual, but was truly comprehensive as to its scope and doctrine.

The simple and central fact is this, that the measure of his woe was the measure of his sense of sin. Artists have sometimes depicted the Pilgrim, setting out from the City of Destruction, as a somewhat debonair saunterer, whose burden is merely a small pack like an extra coat carried by a careful tourist; but to Bunyan the load was a heavy one indeed, and all but insupportable. The grievous distresses of a soul, battling thus with temptation, and at the same time smitten by a paralysing sense of guilt, are without doubt a perennial enigma to Mr. Hold-the-world and Mr. Anything; yet they are the experiences described by the apostle: " O wretched man that I am! who shall deliver me? . . . I thank God through Jesus Christ our Lord." And these experiences were afterwards woven into his great allegory. The man who had agonised to enter in at the strait and narrow " Gap," was the man to portray the Pilgrim as a pitiful but also a determined creature, whose relatives lamented that " some frenzy had got into his head "; but who, while they declared that his burden would sink him to the grave, still ran on, crying: " Life, life, eternal life! "

At the same time, we are not to think of our groaning and praying brasier as pitching a permanent tent " beside the woeful pit of Acheron." Floods of light poured upon his soul. Once in a field, the thought suddenly recurred to him with fresh and convincing force, as though the words had fallen from heaven upon his soul : " Thy righteousness is in heaven." And then, he says : " Methought withal, I saw, with the eyes of my soul, Jesus Christ at God's right hand. I saw, moreover, that it was not my good frame of heart that made my righteousness better, nor yet my bad frame that made my righteousness worse ; for my righteousness was Jesus Christ Himself, ' the same yesterday, and to-day, and for ever.' Now did my chains fall from my legs indeed ; I was loosed from my affliction and irons."

In this thought, and in that other, that Christ " of God is made unto us wisdom, and righteousness, and sanctification, and redemption," he " lived for some time, very sweetly at peace with God through Christ." Thus he was turned from the gruesome spectacle of his own exceeding sinfulness to gaze in rapture upon his Deliverer. " Methought, Christ ! Christ ! There was nothing but Christ that was before my eyes. I could look from myself to Him, and should reckon that all those graces of God that now were green in me, were yet but like those cracked groats and fourpence-halfpennies* that rich men carry in their purses, when their gold is in their trunks at home! Oh, I saw my gold was in my trunk at Home! In Christ, my Lord and Saviour! Now Christ was all; all my wisdom all my righteousness, all my sanctification, and all my redemption."

Subtle temptations did indeed still buzz in his ears; he still had his seasons of tremendous wrestling with unbelief; nevertheless his heart was fixed; his sky was at times overcast, and threatening, but the thunders of the main storm subsided; the Sun of Righteousness had arisen. Now a new trouble threatened him; his health became feeble, and consumption was feared. Whether the illness was caused by overwork and a bare cupboard, or whether mental anguish reacted upon the physical frame, does not appear; perhaps both these were contributory causes; certain it is that he did not expect to live. This crisis led him into solemn reveries on life and death, but in spite of bodily weakness he was

* While "cracked groats" clearly refers to damaged fourpenny pieces, depreciated in value; "fourpence-halfpennies" seems an archaic term. However, Offor, zealous in even the smallest details regarding aught that had to do with Bunyan, has elucidated the point: "What he meant by 'fourpence-halfpennies' somewhat puzzled me, there never having been any piece of English money coined of that value. I found that a proclamation was issued shortly before Mr. Bunyan's time (April 8, 1603) . . . It fixed the value of the Irish twelve-pence piece to be ninepence English; so that the Irish sixpence was to pass current for fourpence-halfpenny in England." The curator of coins at the British Museum, on being consulted by Offor, showed him some of this Irish silver, and agreed that it was doubtless to this coin that Bunyan referred.

D

enabled to draw strength and comfort from Bible promises.

The illness passed. It left him with a treasure of rare experience, a new vision of the glories of heaven and of the spiritual wealth of the heirs of God, a vision so splendid that its loveliness and richness—like that of Paul when " caught up to the third heaven " —could not be uttered in human speech. Yet he strove to tell it : " Now I was got up on high. I saw myself within the arms of Love and Mercy ; and though I was before afraid to think of a dying hour, yet now I cried : ' Let me die ! ' Now death was lovely and beautiful in my sight ; for I saw we shall never live indeed till we be gone to the other world. Oh, methought, this life is but a slumber in comparison of that above ! At this time also I saw more in those words, ' heirs of God,' than ever I shall be able to express while I live in this world. Heirs of God ! God Himself is the portion of His saints. This I saw and wondered at, but cannot tell what I saw."

Thus far had the blaspheming and boisterous mechanic emerged from his darkness ; thus far had he travelled the new and solitary path of spiritual quest, into the peace and quiet of faith. The way he had come was through dark glens and past sudden precipices, but at length he broke through to God. That experiences which seemed so chequered and difficult reminded Bunyan himself of the forty years' wanderings of the Israelites in the wilderness, appears from *Grace Abounding;* but his mind was dwelling, not upon past agony, but upon present deliverance, and upon the path that led still forward. The dusty and scarred pilgrim had come into the Canaan of Divine acceptance in Christ ; now his day of holy service had dawned ; yet, in the fullest sense the Canaan of God was above ; to which he therefore still pressed forward. And in case any should doubt the usefulness of his written confessions, he later declared to his children in the faith his reasons for publishing the sad and solemn record : " If you have sinned against Light ; if you are tempted to blaspheme ; if you are down in despair ; if you think God fights against you ; or if heaven is hid from your eyes, remember it was thus with your father ; but out of them all the Lord delivered me."

Of his domestic life and his trade affairs, Bunyan says little. Probably there was little to chronicle that did not belong to the threadbare annals of the poor, to the everyday round of brasiering and gardening. One pathetic fact, however, stands out vividly ; his eldest child, Mary, was blind.

The rooms of the cottage were small ; Mrs. Bunyan would be glad to get into the garden ; John would be busy in the lean-to workshop ; wherefore no unwarrantable stretch of the imagination is required to think of the struggling workman of Elstow, as sometimes quitting for a moment the fire and the tools, on some hot summer's day, and, stepping from the forge to the garden, breathing a tender consolation to his wife as she tended the cabbages, and kissing the little face of their blind babe lying asleep in the cradle.

III   *Early Activities*

AT the time of Bunyan's conversion, the Authorized Version of the Bible was still a comparatively new force in the land. Apart even from the intense interest of the main body of the people, the personal influence which James I had warmly exercised in its favour had done much to secure its wide circulation, and the prophetic saying of the martyred Tyndale was in a fair way to fulfilment; the Book was coming to be as accessible to the ploughboy, or at any rate to the village pot-mender, as to the priest.

From the Bible, Bunyan drew inspiration to apply his literary gift. It furnished him with subjects of heavenly attraction and profound interest; with an unfailing store of illustration; with a noble model of style. It was from the Bible that his happy homeliness and Anglo-Saxon bluntness, so racy of the soil, won the light and beauty which are such captivating characteristics of his writings.

His manifold conflicts with temptation drove him into close and constant companionship with prophet and psalmist and apostle;

a tenacious memory enabled him to master and marshal passages swiftly; and a nimble wit taught him to use his perseveringly acquired knowledge with aptness and dexterity. His books sparkle with gems of revealed truth; the rubies of Atonement, the diamonds of spiritual light, the amethysts of the Blessed Hope. We well know the mines whence these were dug. They are the mines of the Word of God.

Seeking to join himself with some assembly of Christians with whom he could feel a true sympathy, and being strongly drawn to Gifford and his flock, Bunyan became, in 1653, a member of the little company of believers at Bedford. About this time, too, he was baptised publicly, by Gifford; tradition indicates the spot as being a "natural baptistry" formed by a creek of the Ouse, at the end of what was then Duck Mill Lane, Bedford. Probably in 1655, Bunyan removed from Elstow to Bedford. In the same year Gifford died; and about this time, also, Bunyan's wife passed away, leaving him with blind Mary and three other little ones.

Amid these vicissitudes and labours, however, he still developed in Christian grace and usefulness. Gradually it was recognised that he was highly gifted, alike in exhortation and exposition. The old carnal self-confidence had given place to a sweet modesty and simplicity. When accompanying parties of

Early Activities 55

the saints on preaching expeditions, he would venture an occasional word, but even this was sufficient to reveal the man; such remarkable talents could not remain hidden. Soon, therefore, wherever and whenever he declared the Gospel, throngs of people assembled to hear.

Nor was this surprising, apart from the question of preaching ability, for the conversion of a blaspheming reprobate, well-known to the whole countryside, has ever had an intense interest, from the day of the man who dwelt among the tombs. The common people saw in Bunyan, not some refined dignitary, who, while he might command their esteem, was yet of a different order of society, but a plain man, almost their own flesh and blood, whose language suggested, not the University class-room, but the homespun familiar neighbourliness of the market or the harvest-field; withal, touched with the pathos of one who has prayed and wept in the night watches, yea, and packed with Bible truth and made vital by the Spirit. Such was the new preacher who now emerged into the public life of England.

It was long a fashion in literature to represent such a man—a vigorous convert and a peripatetic preacher of the simple Evangel—as a ranting creature, obsessed with ambitious notions, and tricked out with the odd, fantastical mannerisms of a pronounced vulgarian. This legend, not unnaturally, found favour with the upholders of priestly caste; it moreover supplied comedians like Foote with inexhaustible material for—financially profitable—parody; and its recrudescence in a later day appears in the Dickens' creations of the gross and self-indulgent "shepherd" with a weakness for "pineapple rum," and the howling pulpiteer of the "Little Bethel." We may admit the general scheme to be nominally that of the exposure of hypocrites rather than that of an attack upon humble preachers: but, even so, some authors and comedians have certainly left the impression that their purpose was to gird at unconventional Gospellers, whose aims they did not appreciate and whose value to the community they failed to understand.

Thus it was with the elegants of Bunyan's day. A preaching tinker was a grotesque, whose fitting place would be, by any process of mental classification, outside real life, hobnobbing upon the island with Caliban and Trinculo; while to certain of the ministry, trained according to the school of Laud, he was a sort of clownish "infringement of copyright."

Even in the twentieth century there survives a touch of opprobrium in the association of preaching and pot-mending. People who are tremendously particular to hear only such preachers as they consider "good class," will still regard a Gospelling tinker with contempt, and adapt to the occasion the familiar Johnsonian word : " It is like a dog's walking on his hind legs ; it is not done well, but you are surprised to find it done at all." And if it should be objected, that an adverse judgment is justifiably passed upon any man who pretentiously essays a task for which he is unqualified in ability and unprepared in education, the obvious answer is that no such criticism can apply to Bunyan, for his gifts were splendid, his self-acquired education was drawn chiefly from and through the Bible, his critics were for the most part those who had never heard him, and the magnificent results attending his ministry demonstrated that he was called and anointed of the Holy Ghost.

Moreover, whatever the strange cause that attracted the people, they were enthralled and convicted, not by mere eccentricity, but by ability and sincerity, and above all by the unction and power of the Spirit resting upon the tinker, even in a barn or under a tree in a churchyard. The sot, the gamester, the blasphemer, heard and trembled and wept ; and the poor rejoiced that to them the Gospel was preached. However sourly superior persons might decry him on account of his calling, the instinct of the people swiftly recognised the genius and zeal of the man from the little forge.

The arrows of official arrogance were volleyed at him. The very word " tinker " was found to be mysteriously provocative of sardonic humour. It savoured of the essentially ridiculous. It figured in nursery rhyme, "Tinker, tailor, soldier, sailor." In its association with kitchen implements alone, such a trade was homely even to comicality. Further, it was the favourite alleged employment of gipsy tramps. Shakespeare himself represented a travelling tinker as a drunken boaster and a foolish, ignorant butt. Doubtless, the actual travelling tinker was often ignorant and drunken. All this reproach was thrust upon Bunyan, and furnished, not only the opponents of free Gospel preaching, but all who scorned religion and morality, with a nickname to cast at him—almost a sort of war-whoop.

Prejudice and bitterness and exclusivism are not to be regarded as of one party only ; persecution was not found alone under Laud ; it was to Cromwell himself that George Fox, fresh from his awful experiences in Launceston jail, protested against the persecution of the Friends. With the exception however of one indictment for preaching—which, since nothing came of it, may reasonably be set down to some local misunderstanding or prejudice—Bunyan enjoyed, during the Commonwealth, a large opportunity in the Gospel, of which he fully availed himself. That he grew in fame was a small matter to him ; the ungodly gave heed to the Message of Life ; Christians were edified ; new causes, marked by love for the

Word and consecration to the service of Christ, sprang into being.

Under the broad ecclesiastical system which prevailed between the year 1653 and the Restoration, the assembly at Bedford had found a home in St. John's Church, upon the south side of the Ouse, and close to the spot where Bunyan had listened to the conversation of the godly women. Gifford himself was appointed rector, and his successor was John Burton—also a warm friend of Bunyan's.

These associations assuredly helped to smooth Bunyan's way as a preacher; yet, although the law set no obstacle in his path, the antagonisms of prejudice were bitter. " When I first went to preach the Word," he says, " the doctors and priests of the country did open wide against me. But I was persuaded of this, not to render railing for railing, but to see how many of their carnal professors I could convince of their miserable estate."

The " doctors and priests," on their side, were less considerate. They spared nothing of denunciatory epithet. He was a Jesuit; he was a highwayman. Learned dignitaries and teachers of Cambridge University, into whose neighbourhood he often travelled with the Gospel, were furious. Yet even among themselves there were some who could still delight in a Spirit-taught, humble-minded and heavenly-minded man, who could use the Bible to excellent purpose, as well as manipulate the tools of his daily calling. But in common estimation that calling was inseparable from the man; with high and low alike, he was "the tinker."

While but little disposed to reply to personal attacks, Bunyan found much satisfaction in contending "with great earnestness for the word of faith and the remission of sins by the death and sufferings of Jesus." It was a time of recasting of thought and opinion; moreover, of much liberty of speech. Argumentative collisions regarding points of doctrine and ecclesiastical administration were frequent, and fiery pamphleteering continued the warfare.

We soon find Bunyan engaging in an "earnest contention," for he came warmly into conflict with some of the early Friends, during a vigorous campaign upon which they had entered, in Bedford. Their preaching, he considered, exalted the Inner Light to the injury of his Historical Christ and the written Word. On their side the Friends regarded Bunyan as tending, in his exaltation of the Historical Christ and the written Word, to depreciate somewhat the inward illumination of the Spirit. Quaker enthusiasm was strong, and was fed by the hope of turning many to righteousness, and by the signs of a new spiritual awakening. Bunyan, freshly finding a vent for his volcanic force and looking in faith for a mighty movement among the ungodly, was deeply concerned to maintain a strong and Biblical testimony, free from all obscurity. One typical "Bunyan touch" emerges from the story of his lively personal arguments. In one debate, a Quaker lady bade him, for some reason, "put away his Bible." "No," he at once retorted, "for then the devil would be too hard for me!"

The controversy is noteworthy, because it led to the publication, in 1656, of Bunyan's first book, the characteristic title of which was: *Some Gospel Truths Opened; By that unworthy servant of Christ, John Bunyan, of Bedford, preacher of the Gospel of His dear Son.* An introduction, by Burton, bore witness to the growing esteem in which Bunyan was held. "This man," it said of him, "is not chosen out of an earthly, but out of the heavenly University, the Church of Christ. He hath through grace taken these three heavenly degrees, to wit, union with Christ, the anointing of the Spirit, and experiences of Satan."

The book drew a polemical reply from Edward Burrough, one of the chief of the early Friends, and a zealous and eloquent youth. Bunyan retorted with: *A Vindication of Gospel Truths Opened,* and Burrough hit back; the battle was maintained with vigour, much in the fashion that Baxter charged down upon Baptists and Quakers alike, and they in turn defended themselves and counter-attacked, in a lively pamphleteering warfare. The story of campaigns in book or debate, of one worthy soul against another, may well be left to a quiet repose in the dusty back-cupboards or top shelves of old libraries. The times of freedom to preach were speedily to close. The day was at hand which should bring Bunyan and Burrough and Baxter into a community of suffering long to be remembered. The Protectorate came to an end. Charles II, clasping a Bible to his breast, was welcomed back to England and established on the throne, amid the torrential enthusiasm of apparently the whole nation.

The restoration of the Church of England to its former position was of course inevitable. The old order was once more set up. The bishops yet surviving were reinstated. For a congregation of Independents to remain in possession of St. John's was manifestly impossible. Burton and his flock, like other congregations similarly positioned, had perforce to seek another meeting-place. Moreover, no matter whither they might retire, they would be subject to the severe Elizabethan statute, under which a refusal to attend service at the parish church was an offence punishable by fine; while any who might be found frequenting conventicles, which is to say, "irregular" religious assemblies, were liable to imprisonment, and, in case of persistence, to banishment, the penalty for returning from which, without permission, being—death.

Early Activities

In the autumn of 1660, Burton died. Bunyan, who had been three years a deacon, was now the most prominent man in the little company; indeed he was by sheer force of ability the chief figure, in Bedford and for miles around, among those who conscientiously objected to conform. He was also to be accounted a growing literary power; if not in a high academic sense, at any rate as a forcible and spiritual writer for plain working-folk who were also instructed Christians.

In the graphically-written and terrifyingly-entitled *A Few Signs from Hell; or, the Groans of a Damned Soul*, he had given an exposition of the Parable of the Rich Man and Lazarus, in the course of which he introduced some pungent passages aimed at any who were ensnared by the fear of man, and particularly at the oppressors who set such snares. He said, for instance: "Oh, what red lines will there be against all those rich, ungodly landlords that so keep under their poor tenants that they dare not go out to hear the Word, for fear that their rent should be raised or they turned out of their houses! What sayest thou, landlord, will it not cut thy soul, when thou shalt see that thou couldest not be content to miss of heaven thyself, but thou must labour to hinder others also? Think on this, you drunken, proud, rich, and scornful landlords."

The book was excellent Gospel seed, and

the uncompromising terms of his championship of the poor were truly Bunyanesque. He knew no fear, but such plain-speaking might assuredly arouse the fierce resentment, after the Restoration, of county magnates who had formerly smarted under Commonwealth rule ; but who were now wild with exultation at the long-delayed but sweeping triumph of their party, which had brought them an astonishing opportunity for fully re-establishing their former position of domination, and at the same time furnished them with cruel weapons of reprisal and suppression.

A further work of Bunyan's was entitled : *The Doctrine of the Law and Grace Unfolded*. It was characteristically described in the sub-title as : " A discourse touching the Law and Grace ; the nature of the one and the nature of the other, showing what they are, as they are the two Covenants ; and likewise who they be and what their conditions are, that be under either of these two Covenants : Wherein for the better understanding of the reader, there are several questions answered touching the Law and Grace, very easy to be read, and as easy to be understood by those that are the sons of wisdom, the children of the second Covenant. Published by that poor contemptible creature, John Bunyan, of Bedford."

This little book was an admirable sermon of the Puritan order, plain and understandable. But the " sons of wisdom," reading between the lines, would also comprehend quite clearly that a writer so bold would speedily be found in collision with authority, under any sort of constraining rule that should threaten his freedom to preach the One Mediator and the riches of His grace.

IV The Struggle for Liberty

BUNYAN had not long to wait for the inevitable clash foreshadowed by the collapse of the Commonwealth government. The simple privilege of speaking a word for Jesus Christ in some orchard or kitchen to a little group of humble worshippers became also, in 1660, a dangerous adventure.

William Dell, rector of Yelden and master of Gonville and Caius, Cambridge, found himself the subject of an antagonistic petition to the House of Lords, signed by some Royalists of his parish, which protested that among other objectionable proceedings of his, " Upon Christmas Day, one Bunyan, of Bedford, a tinker, was countenanced and allowed to speak in the pulpit to the congregation." The petition was for some reason dismissed ; but the swiftness with which action was thus taken in the parish was an index of the rising spirit of persecution, for Charles arrived in London on May 29, and the petition was dated June 20.

It would be no difficult matter to find occasion for striking at Bunyan himself. The crisis could not long be postponed in the case of an apostle so dauntless. Active and alert agents were watching him. The justices were ready.

On November 12, he was to preach, by request, at the hamlet of Lower Samsell. On his arrival at the farm-house where the service was to be held, he was told that a warrant had been issued for his arrest. The farmer —perhaps the original of " Mr. Timorous," in the *Pilgrim's Progress*, whose lament was, " the further we go, the more danger we meet with"—suggested that the wiser course would be to dismiss the meeting. Bunyan, however, stoutly bidding the company to be of good cheer, engaged in prayer.

Now entered master constable, bearing the warrant; but the justice—Mr. Francis Wingate, of Harlington House—who had signed it, and before whom the case was to be heard, was away from home for a few hours. On the intervention, therefore, of a friend, Bunyan was released for the night, on the understanding that he would duly surrender to the constable in the morning.

Bunyan fulfilled his undertaking, and was at once taken before Wingate, at Harlington House. The justice was a local magnate, belonging to a well-known Royalist family; and his view of the situation obviously was that, since the king had come into his own again, the " irregular " Gospellers—whose party had filled the regiments that conquered at Marston Moor, and Naseby, and Dunbar, and Worcester—must be put down and preaching rights be vested exclusively in the clergy. The tinker, such magistrates contended, must obey the law; and this meant that he must limit his public activity in religion to attending the parish church; otherwise, there were prisons for law-defiers.

Replying to a sharp question as to why he "did not content himself with his calling," Bunyan defined his objects—"To instruct and counsel people to forsake their sins and close in with Christ, lest they should miserably perish." Further, he declared his ability to "follow his calling, and preach the Word also."

Wingate's retort to this betrayed the animus of the prosecution. In an angry outburst, he growled: "I will break the neck of your meetings." As to bail for the prisoner's appearance at the ensuing quarter-sessions, it could only be granted upon one condition; the preaching must cease. But Bunyan, who had urged others not to compromise, was not the man to make a shameful surrender. He maintained his position. He "would not leave speaking the Word of God." Accordingly, he was set down for committal to jail.

While the warrant was in process of preparation, Bunyan was reviled, on the justice's premises, by the justice's father-in-law, Dr. Lindall, vicar of Harlington, who made some suggestive references to Paul's adversary, Alexander the coppersmith, "aiming, 'tis like at me," says Bunyan, " because I was a tinker." After a spirited conversation, in which the vicar figured but poorly, Bunyan was despatched to jail, in charge of the constable ; but on the way they were stopped by two friends of Bunyan's, who still entertained some hope of arranging the matter with Wingate. Constable and prisoner accordingly waited in the road while these ambassadors proceeded to Harlington House. Presently the well-meaning brethren returned, bearing however the suspicious message that Bunyan should be released, if only he would " say certain words " to the justice.

Unwilling to disoblige his friends, but realising that freedom could only be purchased by betraying his principles, Bunyan, still of course in the constable's charge, returned to the justice's, where he immediately found himself greeted by Wingate's brother-in-law, William Foster. Assuming an appearance of disinterested affection, Foster sought to induce Bunyan to commit himself to a form of words which, while plausibly simple, really stood for a concession of all that Wingate desired. The attempt to cajole, however, proved a complete failure.

Foster next attempted to overcome the prisoner by argument, but it was no difficult matter for Bunyan to meet a debater who, while professing an interest in religion, could yet declare, confusedly : " You make the people neglect their callings ; God has commanded people to work six days, and serve Him on the seventh." "It is the duty of people," replied the prisoner, " to look out for their souls as well as their bodies ; and God would have his people ' exhort one another daily, while it is called To-day.' " Foster strove to maintain an argument. Obviously, it was not desirable that a man of education and position should be routed in debate, but the more he said the worse his predicament became. At length he took refuge in belittling the character of Bunyan's congregations. " None come to hear you " he urged, " but a company of poor, simple, ignorant people." " It is the foolish and ignorant," Bunyan calmly replied, " who have most need of teaching and information, and therefore it will be profitable for me to go on in that work."

The feeble arguments of Foster having proved altogether ineffective, nothing remained but to consign the rebellious tinker to jail ; and there at length the constable deposited him. His stout heart failed not, through grace. The thought of his children might well have caused the tears to well up, but even in this matter there was compensating reason for thankfulness. The death of his wife, as we have seen, had left him with four little children to care for. The position was a difficult one. His calling often took him from home, on duties of fetching and carrying. To bring in a housekeeper would be both expensive and provocative of tittle-tattle. Wisely therefore, he had married a second wife, a godly woman who carefully tended the motherless little mites, and was in every way a tower of strength to her husband. He could therefore rest confident that blind Mary and the rest were in the best possible care.

In any case, his hope was in God: even in the prison he wrote: " I lie waiting the good will of God, to do with me as He pleaseth ; knowing that not one hair of my head can fall to the ground without the will of my Father which is in Heaven. Let the rage and malice of men be never so great, they can do no more, nor go no further, than God permits them ; but when they have done their worst, ' we know that all things work together for good to them that love God.'"

The records of judicial proceedings, under the Protectorate, but chiefly in the black days between the Restoration and the Revolution, possess a fascinating interest which lies, not in luminous disquisitions from the bench, but in the admirable spirit in which, in defence of the right to witness for Christ and His Gospel, the persecuted saints quietly met the furious hectoring of unjust judges, and ably answered the preposterous charges formulated under laws deliberately framed to accomplish the repression of religious freedom.

Ermined authority, when divorced from

justice, revealed its weakness more particularly when attempting to silence a prisoner, not only by browbeating abuse, but, in a spirit of astonishing presumption, by arguments professedly founded upon the Bible. In so doing the bench placed itself at an enormous disadvantage. If the judges could justify the law on no sound principle of equity, they could at least plead that it was their business, not to justify but to administer. But when they strove to support unjust laws by appeals to Scripture they were figuratively in the position of Leslie at Dunbar, needlessly venturing into an exposed situation, and inviting the onslaught of the enemy. Such victims of repressive legislation as Bunyan and George Fox were more than a match for the malignant and revengeful dignitaries before whom they were dragged, alike in ability as in knowledge; and they poured such a raking fire of exposition and retort upon the unhappy judges that, practically, the prisoner became the prosecutor, and the Bench, in the estimation of unprejudiced people were the real malefactors.

Bunyan's stand was in no sense political; it was purely Christian. He sought no quarrel; the attack came from the side of repression. And the fatal weakness of that side was, politics altogether apart, that in seeking to secure political results it condemned as illegal the proclamation of the message of redeeming love. To deliver that message to all mankind was a duty which the Founder of Christianity made incumbent upon all His people, since they were to be His witnesses.

The struggle in which Bunyan was involved was therefore essentially one between human authority and Divine ; and it was scarcely to be supposed that the tinker, with love and gratitude to God upspringing in his soul, would hesitate in a choice between the sweet injunctions of the Shepherd of Israel and those of the law of England as dictated by Clarendon, and interpreted by party zealots of the type of Mr. Francis Wingate, of Harlington House, and his father-in-law and brother-in-law.

The actual charge against Bunyan was formulated under the Elizabethan statute, but to urge this as an apology for the arrest is to make but a poor attempt at the exculpation of the magistrates or the Government. Clarendon was in power, although a few months had to elapse before the new laws could be introduced. Meantime, it was at least possible to revive the angry legislation of the Tudor times, and this was done, not however from any regard for the majesty of the law, but in order to lose no time in putting down the detested conventicles.

Something might assuredly have been looked for in the way of retaliation, for the repressive laws of the Protectorate which, by preventing the dispossessed clergyman from preaching or teaching, practically deprived him of the means of livelihood. Much might also be conceded to the honest suspicion that the conventicle might be used as a cover for the gathering of seditious persons with treasonable purposes in view. But the alleged fear of a rebellion was ordinarily nothing more than a specious excuse for putting down prayer-meetings and harrying humble groups of sincere worshippers whose only weapon was the Sword of the Spirit. Moreover, the Declaration of Breda, issued by Charles just prior to the Restoration —and avowedly as a manifesto to prepare the way for that event—promised that no man should be disquieted for differences of opinion in religion that did not disturb the peace of the Kingdom.

Doubtless the king was less to blame than his counsellors. Although the sacrifice of his word was a small matter to him, and although he held quite distinctly that, for example, Presbyterianism was "no religion for a gentleman," he would not seek trouble if only he could in peace finance in an adequate way the indulgences of Whitehall. The party spirit of his own supporters, however, was too strong for him. The Cavaliers had suffered keenly and long. Now was their time, if not for revenge for the past, at least for rigorous repression in the present, as a guarantee, it might be hoped, for the future.

To be exact, the indictment which Bunyan was to answer at the quarter sessions charged him with " devilishly and perniciously abstaining from coming to Church to hear Divine Service, and for being a common upholder of several unlawful meetings and conventicles, to the great disturbance and distraction of the good subjects of this kingdom, contrary to the laws of our sovereign lord the king."

The character of the bench suggested an array of expectant cats assembled to consider, judicially and impartially, the obvious misdemeanours of an especially fine mouse. Two of the justices, as Dr. Brown shows, had just been knighted ; the name of another appeared a little later in the Coronation " Honours List " ; a fourth was subsequently made sheriff of the county ; the fifth was that forbidding person, Sir John Kelynge, who, after having suffered much under the Commonwealth, was now beginning to reap the reward of loyalty and endurance. He was embarking, with the patronage and help of Clarendon, upon a career which was to culminate in his being made Lord Chief Justice ; but he was extremely sour and arbitrary ; even his friends tired of his harsh and insolent spirit ; at this time he was a serjeant-at-law.

The prisoner's mild and sensible replies, in a close argument with Kelynge, only irritated the rest of the Bench. One magistrate urged that the prisoner should be silenced forthwith ; another demanded of him, " Whether his God was Beelzebub ? " A frequent suggestion was, that he was " possessed of the devil."

But neither browbeating nor insults moved him; the cry of his heart was: "The Lord forgive them!"

The debate with Kelynge produced no magisterial advantage; the matter was summed up in Bunyan's godly protestation: "Blessed be the Lord for it, we are encouraged to meet together, and to pray, and to exhort one another; for we have the comfortable presence of God among us: for ever blessed be His holy Name!" This salted speech was a foreign tongue to Kelynge, who styled it "pedlar's French," and, bidding Bunyan "leave off canting," demanded to know by what authority he preached. The argument proceeded thus:

Bunyan: "I will prove that it is lawful for me, and for such as I am, to preach the Word of God."

Kelynge: "By what Scripture?"

Bunyan: "By that in the First Epistle of Peter, the fourth chapter, the tenth verse; and Acts, the eighteenth chapter; and——"

Kelynge: "Hold! Not so many! Which is the first?"

Bunyan: "This: 'As every man hath received the gift, even so let him minister the same one to another, as good stewards of the manifold grace of God. If any man speak, let him speak as the oracles of God; if any man minister, let him do it as of the ability which God giveth.'"

The justice now ventured into the field of Bible exposition :

Kelynge : " Let me a little open that Scripture to you : 'As every man hath received the gift '—that is, as every man hath received a trade, so let him follow it. If any man have received a gift of tinkering as thou hast done, let him follow his tinkering ; and so other men their trades ; and the divine, his calling."

Bunyan : " Nay, sir, but it is most clear, that the apostle speaks of preaching the Word. If you do but compare the verses together, the next verse explains this gift, what it is, saying : ' If any man speak, let him speak as the oracles of God.' So that it is plain, that the Holy Ghost doth not so much in this place exhort to civil callings, as to the exercising of those gifts that we have received from God."

Kelynge : " We may do it in families, but not otherwise."

Bunyan : " If it is lawful to do good to *some*, it is lawful to do good to *more*. If it is a good duty to exhort our families, it is good to exhort others ; but if you hold it a sin to meet together to seek the face of God, and exhort one another to follow Christ, I shall ' sin ' still, for so we should do."

At this, Kelynge admitted his inability to pursue the matter, as he was not sufficiently versed in Scripture ; moreover, the Bench would wait no longer; and Bunyan's plain assertions seemed sufficient admission.

"Then you confess the indictment, do you not?" demanded Kelynge. Passing over this endeavour to draw him into an absolute admission of law-breaking, Bunyan retorted with the simple confession of fact: "This I confess," he declared of the assemblies of the saints, "that we have had many meetings together, both to pray to God, and to exhort one another, and that we have had the sweet, comforting presence of the Lord among us for our encouragement; blessed be His name therefore."

Such was the crime, such was the prisoner; such were the justices. The sentence was three months imprisonment; with contingencies: a subsequent refusal to attend church and to cease preaching would mean banishment; further, should he, in such an event, return without a licence, he should, in Kelynge's phrase, "stretch by the neck for it."

The tinker remained undaunted, declaring: "If I were out of prison to-day, I would preach the Gospel again to-morrow, by the help of God." The jailer pulled him away, and he was taken back to the county prison. He went in peace, his testimony being: "I bless the Lord Jesus Christ for it, that my heart was sweetly refreshed at the time of my examination, and also afterwards, at my returning to the prison. So that I found

Christ's words more than bare trifles, where He saith He will give a mouth and wisdom, even such as all the adversaries shall not resist or gainsay; and that His peace no man can take from us."

Mrs. Bunyan had been sore stricken at the news of her husband's arrest; within a few days a little one was born to them; but the tiny flower was swiftly transplanted into the garden of God.

About three months later, the justices, possibly moved by the wide sympathy with Bunyan, made a further attempt to persuade him to submit, sending the Clerk of the Peace as their ambassador, but in arguing so unrighteous a case the Clerk was no better equipped than Foster, or Kelynge himself. Bunyan outmatched his visitor alike in Scripture as in common sense; and—a fact suggestive of his progress in scholarship since the wild days of folly—he very aptly quoted a saying of Wickliffe, that "he that leaveth off preaching and hearing the Word of God, for fear of being excommunicated of men, is already excommunicated of God, and shall in the Day of Judgment be counted a traitor to Christ."

The discussion did not advance matters. The three months sentence was served. Bunyan had not submitted, but Kelynge and his fellow-justices were content to take no further action.

In connection with the Coronation, which

took place on April 23, three weeks after the conversation between Bunyan and the Clerk of the Peace, many prisoners were released from the various jails of the Kingdom, in accordance with the exercise of royal clemency customary upon such an occasion, but the list of names had to be approved by the local authority. Bunyan was still detained. By proclamation, a twelvemonth was allowed during which the recommendations might be made; but the justices were obviously determined to insist on his submission. He was simply left in jail.

Yet he did not lack an earnest champion. Mrs. Bunyan clearly did not derive from the despairing line of the Despondencys, but from the sturdy stock of the Standfasts. She determined, courageous country woman that she was, to go to London and plead personally for justice for her husband. It was no easy matter to enlist the help of the mighty at such a moment, for a despised and persistent conventicle Gospeller. Nevertheless, a kindly peer, Lord Barkwood, received a petition from Mrs. Bunyan, and called the attention of other members of the House to it. As a result, the heroine of humble life was assured that the peers were not themselves qualified to issue an order of release, but that they had referred the matter to the judges, for consideration at the ensuing assizes. This indeed was but cold comfort, but she could accomplish no more for the moment.

Mrs. Bunyan accordingly returned to Bedford, and awaited the arrival of the two judges, Twisden and Sir Matthew Hale. The assize was held in August, 1661. Bunyan had prepared a petition in which he asked to be heard, and to have his case considered; and his wife proceeded to present it to the judges. Very wisely, she first approached Hale, who bore a well-deserved reputation for mildness on the bench in a day when mildness was apt to be regarded as something akin to disloyalty; and of whom Baxter said: "I believe he would have lost all he had in the world rather than do an unjust act."

Hale received the humble suppliant with kindness, but expressed a fear that he could take no legal action. On the next day, Mrs. Bunyan threw a petition into the coach in which Twisden was being taken from the Swan Inn to the court. The judge glanced through the petition, but waspishly remarked that Bunyan was "a convicted person, who could not be released unless he gave an undertaking to preach no more."

Yet again, in the court itself, Mrs. Bunyan presented a petition, addressing herself to Hale; but Sir Henry Chester, one of the Bench by whom the original conviction was pronounced, broke out into a denunciation of Bunyan as being "a hot-spirited fellow" who stood duly convicted. Hale, doubtless quite convinced that he could do nothing, under the law, took no action.

Mrs. Bunyan was still undismayed; this undaunted daughter of the peasantry, acting upon a hint from Edward Wylde, the high sheriff, made her way into the large chamber at the Swan, where Hale and Twisden were receiving the county gentry. She sought to know, from Hale, what was to be done about her husband's case. Chester hastily interrupted again, to the effect that Bunyan had been lawfully convicted; but Hale, after eliciting from Mrs. Bunyan some pathetic particulars of her domestic trials—her bereavement, and her struggle with poverty, ejaculated: "Alas, poor woman!" He then called for the statute book; and meanwhile advised his poor suppliant that she must either apply to the king or sue out a pardon or obtain a writ of error.

Hale's considerate attitude was in sharp contrast with the petulant intolerance of the rest. Twisden—whose narrow temper also appears in sundry lively court arguments with George Fox, in which the prisoner's knotty law and sound Gospel greatly irritated the judge—offered the miserable suggestion that Bunyan had found it more profitable, financially, to preach than to "follow his calling."

At this Hale enquired, in all simplicity; "What *is* his calling?" The information was easily elicited. Probably every man in the company, whether a plain home-loving squire or a devotee of the dice in London gambling houses, was aware of Bunyan's trade. Several at once replied: "A tinker, my lord!" "Yes," cried his wife, "and because he is a tinker, and a poor man, he is despised and cannot have justice."

That Hale should indicate to the tinker's wife a possible course of legal action was gall to Chester, who moreover was well acquainted with Bunyan's indomitable spirit. "My lord," he insisted, "he will preach and do what he lists"; to which Mrs. Bunyan sturdily replied: "He preacheth nothing but the Word of God." This was too much for Twisden; the notion of a tinker preaching, and of the tinker's wife demanding from the judges of assize and the county gentry: "Let my husband go!" set his anger aflame. Making towards the poor woman as though he would strike her, he wrathfully cried: "He 'preach the Word of God!' He runneth up and down doing harm."

Whether the vitriolic judge meant to convey an allusion to Satan "going to and fro in the earth" is not clear; but Mrs. Bunyan would allow no perversion of truth; she replied: "My lord, God hath owned him and done much good by him."

Twisden was aghast. "*God?*" he echoed. And with a smack of Bible phrase which he had perhaps acquired on circuit, from persecuted saints, he added: "His doctrine is of the devil."

The argument now resolved itself into a

final duel between Twisden and his unflinching opponent. The scene and the language naturally carry a reminder of the wife of John Welch, of Ayr, the daughter of John Knox, defending the cause of her husband and her father against the angry and vituperative king of Scots. With similar womanly dignity and godly sincerity, Mrs. Bunyan made reply to her intolerant critic, saying: "My lord, when the Righteous Judge shall appear, it will be known that his doctrine is not the doctrine of the devil."

It may have been that Twisden felt some twinge of conscience, or it may simply have been that the assize dinner was waiting; in any case he appealed to Hale, saying: "My lord, send her away." But Hale would be discourteous to none. Turning to Mrs. Bunyan, he expressed his sorrow that under the law he could see no way by which to help her to obtain an immediate discharge. Then he reiterated his former advice, saying: "A writ of error will be cheapest."

Chester was now irritated beyond words, that the judge should again advise the tinker's wife, for the benefit of the tinker. With a gesture of irrepressible impatience he pulled off his hat and—so Mrs. Bunyan thought—"scratched his head for anger."

There was however no more to be said, and she withdrew. Tears were in her eyes as she threaded her way out through the distinguished company. But, as became a servant of Him to whom the formalists in His own earthly day said : " Say we not truly, Thou hast a devil," they were tears, not of chagrin but of sorrow in thinking, as she said : " What a sad account such poor creatures will have to give at the Coming of the Lord, when they shall there answer for all things whatsoever they have done in the body, whether it be good or whether it be bad."

V   *Bedford Jail*

No attempt was made by Bunyan to carry the case to a higher authority. Apart from all other considerations, poverty and the family circumstances and troubles would prohibit further effort in London. There were indeed points of *prima facie* importance to submit. It might well have been contended that he had never directly pleaded to the indictment, that no evidence had been tendered against him, and that his trial was really no more than a conversation between the justices and himself, his remarks being arbitrarily set down as an admission of having broken the law.

Yet, as Bunyan himself fully realised, the essential position was that of The Tinker versus The State. In maintaining his fundamental right to proclaim the Gospel, and to take part in whatsoever Christian assemblies he chose, he was indeed obeying the commands conveyed to him through the Bible, but he was defying the British Government. And even if an appeal against the justices' inaction proved successful, or even if a "pardon" were obtained, his fixed resolution still to preach the Gospel could only have one result. No "pardon," no reversal of judgment, no writ of error could bring more than a few days freedom to the man who fought single-handed against all the authority of the land.

Following the assizes, Bunyan was allowed a measure of liberty which is somewhat difficult to understand, unless indeed the high sheriff, who, as we have seen had showed kindness to Mrs. Bunyan, permitted it on the ground that the twelve-month during which the prisoner might sue for pardon was unexpired, and that in view of this some latitude might be allowed. That the jailer himself was warmly sympathetic seems quite clear.

Freedom was for Bunyan simply an opportunity to make known the Gospel, and to declare the unsearchable riches of Christ. He pursued his usual course of "visiting the people of God." Upon one occasion, he went so far afield as London, but, the fact becoming known, the jailer was threatened with dismissal and indictment, and the prisoner's brief span of comparative liberty came suddenly to an end; at most it could have lasted only a few months, as his narrative shows.

He fully anticipated being tried at the sessions of November, 1661, and expected, he says, to be " roundly dealt with " thereat, but he was passed over, the intention obviously being, simply to leave him in jail for an indefinite period. Practically he was under a sentence of, " Stay where you are until you submit "—which submission, to him, meant betraying Christ, and selling, for mere personal liberty, the glorious privileges of apostleship to which he was called of God. Submit, he would not.

The assizes of January, 1662, were now approaching, and Bunyan resolved to press for a regular trial. To this end he endeavoured to have his name entered in the calendar of offenders. The jailer made no difficulty but inserted the name. The sheriff, also, promised that Bunyan should be brought up. The Clerk of the Peace, however, working in harmony with the justices, altered the entry so that instead of appearing as a charge to be heard, it stated that Bunyan was a lawfully-convicted prisoner.

Thus, he was still left in jail, where he remained for six years, when, according to the anonymous *Continuation of Mr. Bunyan's Life*, which in 1692 was appended to *Grace Abounding*, he was released " by the intercession of some trust and power that took pity on his sufferings." The version of the matter given by Charles Doe, a London comb-maker, who, during the last three years of Bunyan's life, came to know him and to be his devoted friend and admirer, is: " He was let out again, 1666, being the year of the burning of London, and, a little after his release, they took him again at a meeting, and put him in the same jail, where he lay six years more."

As we have seen, Bunyan was first arrested, November 12, 1660; his pardon under the Great Seal was issued, September 13, 1672, the actual release, however, may have taken place somewhat earlier in that year, as Dr. Brown suggests, since his " licence to teach " the Nonconformist congregation at Bedford was dated May 9.

At times the prison rules were relaxed somewhat, so that he was occasionally allowed out, on parole; nevertheless, after giving due weight to the fact that concessions were made such as the political situation might suggest to the justices, or humanity and confidence might inspire a jailer or a sheriff to permit, the bitter fact remains that a humble-minded and godly English mechanic, of extraordinary force of intellect and brilliance of imagination, and desiring neither honours nor emoluments, was held in more or less rigid imprisonment for that long period of years for no other offence than an insistence upon the elementary right of the Christian citizen of a free country to worship God in the way his conscience may approve; to testify as he may be led, to the grace and love and power that are in Christ; and to preach the everlasting Gospel.

To appreciate Bunyan's attitude towards constituted authority it is desirable to recall the circumstances of the time, albeit remembering that the embers of the old controversy glowed angrily still. The most careful chroniclers have still found themselves exposed to the suspicion of partisanship, if, although they have striven to hold the balances with rigid impartiality, the scale has seemed to turn but in the estimation of a hair.

In Clarendon, the ascendant party possessed a leader whose experience in statecraft, together with his uncompromising adherence to the old school of Cavaliers, admirably equipped him for the task of formulating and carrying through Parliament such legislation as would consolidate their position of dominance, and thus complete their triumph. And their conception of such legislation was, like his own, one of compulsion, not of conciliation.

The outcome of their efforts was the series of laws called the Clarendon Code. The Act of Uniformity, of 1662, while settling the question of the government of the Church of England upon the basis of Episcopacy, and therefore adversely to the Presbyterian views held by numerous excellent clergymen who hoped for a scheme of wide toleration within the pale of the Establishment, could not fail to provoke new controversy, and at the same time to force into being new and separate causes. For it was not possible that those who, for whatsoever reason, objected to conform, would cease their Christian testimony or stay their endeavours to turn sinners to God. They would still be breaking the bread of life, if not in the old, familiar church, then, like Bunyan, in a farm-house or a barn; their psalm of praise would be raised, if not under a stately cathedral roof, by all means beside the willows of the brook.

All this, Clarendon failed to understand; or, understanding, scorned. There was one State: there must be one Church. The rule must be rigid: the penalties for law-breakers such as would crush them utterly into submission or weed them out of the nation. These theories were the theories of the hour, and they were speedily and fiercely translated into action. The rule was made rigid, indeed, and the penalties crushing. But mediæval and Tudor methods of dealing could no longer be applied with success. Even in the days of Gardiner and Bonner, it had been demonstrated that the conscience could not be arbitrarily controlled by laws and rulers. It is not to be urged that Clarendon sought, according to his lights, to buttress spiritual religion, even by punitive legislation. His aims were mainly political. They failed. He might fill the treasury with fines and the prisons with men and women, but he could not break the spirit of humble Christians contending for Christian freedom.

As for Charles, he was not likely, unless in the interests of Roman Catholicism, to quarrel with the warmly-held opinions of his own supporters, who had just brought him back in triumph from exile and poverty to Whitehall, as to the extent to which they might harry the party of conventicle and of incipient rebellion. And, since the conventicle people had always professed so great a fondness for Parliamentary rule, let them accept that ripe product of Parliament, the Clarendon Code. To differentiate between the loyal and the disloyal among Baptists and Quakers and Independents and Presbyterians was too difficult and thorny a task for Charles; to unite the nation, and apply the cleansing and healing balms of love and tenderness to the old wounds, was beyond the skill of a medicine-man so dilatory; moreover his scrip was empty—or contained only a bottle of French brandy and a dice box.

The ancient distrusts, then, were to survive; were indeed to be endued with fresh life and vigour. To the victors, as it had been under the Protectorate, belonged the spoils. The Conventicle Act, of 1684, declared conventicles—which is to say, any religious services other than those of the Church of England—to be seditious; wherefore any person over the age of sixteen convicted of attending a prayer-meeting at which more than five people were present, became liable to a fine or three months imprisonment. The sentence for a second offence could be a fine or six months imprisonment; for a third, transportation for seven years.

Failing to realise that in such matters force is no remedy, legislators struck a further blow. Under the Five Mile Act, of 1665, no dissenting minister—and all the clergy excluded by the Act of Uniformity were of necessity Nonconformists—might, "except only in passing upon the road," approach within five miles of any place where he had formerly preached or taught, unless he would take the oath of non-resistance ; neither might he act as a schoolmaster. The penalty under this Act was, a fine of £40 and six months imprisonment.

The natural outcome of the Code was the crowding of prisons with Christian men and women, who sought no quarrel, and desired only to be left in peace to their own religious assemblies and their own way of worship, but who would suffer the loss of all things rather than forego rights which they held sacred.

The condition of the country became mournful indeed, and it was small comfort to reflect that Independents and Presbyterians were now tasting the same diet as that with which they had regaled the Episcopalians under the Commonwealth. The basal trouble was that the Code brought the State into collision with what even so formal a religionist as Wellington, later called "the marching orders" of the Church of Christ, to proclaim the Gospel to every creature.

Under these sweeping enactments,

thousands of godly people perished in jail. Numbers were transported—practically as slaves. A member of the Established Church was at the pains to collect a list of names of those who suffered by fine or imprisonment : the total was more than sixty-eight thousand. And while the country was thus ravaged afresh by a policy of coercion in the realm of conscience, the king sold Dunkirk to the French for £400,000 ; and, by the treaty of Dover, agreed to declare himself a Roman Catholic, and to support the Continental designs of Louis XIV, in return for a pension of £200,000 a year, and a promise of the aid of French troops in case of a rebellion at home.

Bunyan, then, was one of a vast family of the persecuted. When the Clarendon Code came to be administered, and fresh prisoners were brought into the jail, he enjoyed Christian fellowship with them ; but his definite decision to preach for Christ wheresoever he found opportunity, despite all manmade laws, was a personal determination. Even if he had to spend all his days in dungeons, he would still stand for Christ, refusing to recognise any enactment by which the Gospel was to be hid.

His position has not escaped the sarcasm or condescending correction of distinguished critics. Froude, discounting any " eloquent declamation " upon the subject of the imprisonment, urges that " it might have ended at any time if he would have promised to confine his addresses to a private circle." Such a view, however, seems to betray the fundamental failure of even the acutest agnosticism to grasp the meaning of Christian and Christian testimony.

Again Garnet echoes Froude by saying of Bunyan : " He might have obtained liberty by a trifling submission." Which is to say that, being called of God to preach the Gospel and having in his hand the open Book of Instruction in the Christian life, he should have scorned the Heavenly command, sold his birthright, trodden the Book under foot, and turned his back upon the cross and the Redeemer, in compliance with the statesmanlike counsels of Mr. Worldly Wiseman and of Mr. Turnaway, that dwelt in the town of Apostasy.

Such a course might conceivably have been suggested to Paul by Agrippa, but we know with what effect. Nor indeed, as the story of Ahab and Micaiah may remind us, was it a novel thing for authority to say to a prophet who declined to join the company of men-pleasers : " Put this fellow in prison and feed him with the bread of affliction." But to imagine that a fundamental principle may be abandoned because the betrayal may be accomplished by an action or word that is in itself trivial, is merely to translate into modern terms the ancient invitation to cast just a grain of incense to Diana. Bunyan could endure, by the grace of God, albeit with pangs and tears, the weary years of durance, but he could not stoop to betray his Lord by a shameful surrender.

The place of his imprisonment was the county jail, which stood at the northern corner of the junction of Silver Street—or Gaol Lane, as it was called at that time—with High Street. The terrors of the prison have occasionally been too strongly pictured by sympathetic but too imaginative chroniclers, and this has provoked critical suggestions to the effect that the prison life was by no means of a trying character.

Nevertheless, while not exactly a pest house, like some of the foul dens in which not a few Christians were done to death in that dark period, it is by no means to be spoken of, as some comments might almost lead us to think, in the terms of an estate agent's catalogue of desirable residences, nor must a controversy as to the details detract our attention from the main fact, that for over eleven years the man of God was the victim for conscience sake, of cruel and repressive laws.

The truth regarding the prison lies midway between the two extremes. John Howard had not yet arisen; a sense of national responsibility for maintaining a spirit of humanity in prison administration was not yet created. When, a century later, Howard's noble career of philanthropy began, he first dealt with this very jail, of which, particularly as he was high sheriff of the county, he was well able to give an exact description. His record tells us that on the ground floor, which was devoted to felons, there were two day rooms and a sleeping room, and on the upper floor, or debtors' section, four sleeping rooms and a day room, which also served the purpose of jail chapel. All the prisoners shared the privileges of a wretched little courtyard. Two underground dungeons completed the accommodation. One forbidding relic of the prison, an interior door, is still preserved at Bedford; it speaks convincingly of the character of the jail which was for those long years the home of John Bunyan.

The spirit in which he endured was truly that of a heavenly-minded apostle. His triumph was in God; his consolation was in prayer and the Bible, and in unfolding the Gospel to his fellow-prisoners. His testimony was: "I never had, in all my life, so great an inlet into the Word of God as now; those Scriptures that I saw nothing in before, are made in this place and state to shine upon me. Jesus Christ also was never more real and apparent than now; here I have seen Him and felt Him indeed. Oh, that word: 'We have not preached unto you cunningly devised fables'; and that: 'God raised Christ up from the dead and gave Him glory; that your faith and hope might be in God,' were blessed words unto me in this my imprisoned condition. These three or four Scriptures also have been great refreshment to me: John xiv. 1–4; John xvi. 33; Col. iii. 3; and Heb. xii. 22–24, so that sometimes, when I have been in the savour of them, I have been able to laugh at destruction, and to fear neither 'the horse nor his rider.'"

The reference to "destruction" was no mere empty use of the phrase. In the earlier days of his imprisonment he was facing the thought that "my imprisonment might end at the gallows, for aught that I could tell"; and an anxious fear oppressed him for a time lest, by betraying timorousness when climbing the ladder to be hanged, he might bring reproach upon the people of God. "Wherefore," he says, "I prayed to God that He would comfort me, and give me strength to do and suffer what he should call me to."

A touch of his old agony, of God being hidden from him, settled momentarily upon his soul; but he arose to conquer, crying: "I am for going on, and venturing my eternal state with Christ, whether I have comfort here or no; if God doth not come in (thought I) I will leap off the ladder even blindfold into eternity, sink or swim, come heaven, come hell; Lord Jesus, if Thou wilt catch me, do; 'if not,' I will venture on Thy name." The "if not" seems to suggest that he had in mind the "if not" of Shadrach, Meshach and Abednego: "Our God whom we serve will deliver us. . . . But 'if not' . . . we will not serve thy gods, nor worship the golden image."

Yet, while finding comfort in the thought of venturing wholly on God, his heart was sorely grieved at the forlorn and bereft state of his heroic wife and the children. To leave them was like " pulling the flesh off his bones." That he was himself deprived of home and liberty was a matter to be borne with; but his soul was torn indeed in thinking of the hardships that his family must face— especially, as being the most helpless, blind Mary.

Bunyan's lament for his blind daughter is a poignant human cry, sounding down to us from the darkness of those wretched times, and touching the heart. "Poor child, thought I, what sorrow art thou like to have for thy portion in this world! Thou must be beaten, must beg, suffer hunger, cold, nakedness, and a thousand calamities, though I cannot now endure the wind should blow upon thee. But yet, recalling myself, thought I, I must venture you all with God, though it goeth to the quick to leave you. Oh, I saw in this condition I was as a man who was pulling down his house upon the head of his wife and children; yet, thought I, I must do it, I must do it."

Amid these agonising thoughts of the desolate home, three main considerations inspired him to a fresh flight of faith in behalf of his loved ones, and to a yet more glowing determination to "trust, and not be afraid." The first was the commandment and promise of Jer. xlix. 11, "Leave thy fatherless children, I will preserve them alive; and let thy widows trust in Me"; the second, the promise of Jer. xv. 11, "The Lord said, Verily it shall be well with thy remnant; verily I will cause the enemy to entreat thee well in the time of evil"; and the third, to use his own words: "this consideration, that if I should venture all for God, I engaged God to take care of my concernments; but if I forsook Him and His ways, for fear of any trouble that should come to me or mine, then I should not only falsify my profession, but should count also that my concernments were not so sure, if left at God's feet, while I stood to and for His name, as they would be, if they were under my own tuition, though with the denial of God."

Even in so melancholy an abode as Bedford jail, Bunyan thus showed an indomitable spirit. He wrote book after book, and toiled indefatigably for the support of his family. Brasiering being out of the question, he turned to other pursuits. An anonymous writer, who evidently knew him well, declares that, far from spending the time in a supine and careless manner, or eating the bread of idleness, Bunyan was highly industrious, "for" says this writer, "I have been witness that his own hands have ministered to his and his family's necessities, making many hundred gross of long-tagged laces, to fill up the vacancies of his time, which he had learned for that purpose since he had been in prison."

Christian brotherliness, as well as regard for Bunyan as a persecuted witness for Christ, and sympathy for his wife and children, would doubtless lead the saints at Bedford to give such practical help as their cramped resources would allow; but they were themselves being brought under the harrow of the Clarendon Code. Bedford jail was crammed with prisoners, both men and women. Some of Bunyan's fellow-members were there. The spirit of religious liberty could not be crushed; despite the law, people would still meet to praise God and beseech His blessing, and edify one another in the truth; but their persistence was sternly met. They were spied upon, arrested, and imprisoned; or reduced almost to beggary.

Further the law was made still more oppressive, by the second Conventicle Act, of 1670. And if the law itself was savage, much more so was the spirit of its administration. The stipulation that the third part of every fine should go to the informer gave fresh encouragement to the most debased of men, to become sleuth-hounds for hunting down people of prayerful, Bible-loving life, who happened to have difficulties of conscience regarding the Clarendon Acts, and who still sought to meet together in the name of the Lord. Justices who failed to carry out the law were themselves to be punished; and a Bishop threatened that a yet stronger law would be passed, under which offenders should not only be deprived of their land and goods, but should be sold as slaves.

So fiercely was the second Conventicle Act carried out that the sums extorted in fines and confiscations amounted to a vast total. Many industrious persons, representing also some of the best elements of the community, were stripped of their savings and indeed of their all. Foster—who had pretended to a friendly interest in Bunyan—and other justices spoiled the conventicle-going Christians of Bedfordshire, in a new sway of despotism; and what was true regarding Bedfordshire was equally true of the rest of the country; justices and constables and spies were full of zeal, and the military forces were to be used in the work of suppression if the Lieutenants of counties thought it desirable.

The chief results of this dragonnade were, apart from the mere financial gains, the gratifying of political hatreds, the intensifying of religious differences, and the enriching of a horde of drunken and blasphemous sharpers of the order typified in a later day by Mr. Sampson Brass and Mr. Roger Cly.

The details that are available, of Bunyan's prison life, are but few. Indeed the whole record of these years is provokingly obscure.

During some parts of the time he was occasionally allowed out on parole, as appears from the records of the church meetings, wherein the fact of his attendance is recorded; but for seven years, from October, 1661, to October, 1668, there is no mention of his name. It seems from the statement of one of his friends, that he was sometimes " under cruel and oppressive gaolers"; then, again, upon his being rearrested, in 1668, he was, at any rate for a time, much more kindly treated, for " the gaoler took such pity of his rigorous sufferings that he did as the Egyptian gaoler did to Joseph, put all care and trust into his hands."

Between October, 1668, and the passing of the second Conventicle Act, in 1670, Bunyan was frequently deputed by the church to act in such duties as admonishing those members who, under the stress of fierce persecution, fell away to what the church books call " the world's way of worship"; and instructing converts. And his signature appears, with three others, at the end of a letter addressed to several of the churches in the country, advising them of the evil conduct of one who, as well as committing other serious offences, " went in the name of the church, particularly naming Joh. Bunyan and Sam ffenne, and yet wholly without their knowledge or consent, to beg the charity of ye good people of St. Neots."

Bunyan's literary gift became of particular

service in the drawing up of letters of sympathy and encouragement, to be sent to the persecuted ones of the district. These missives were usually signed by the two ffennes—or Fenns, Samuel and John, hatmakers and haberdashers, of Bedford—and others, including Bunyan himself: they were touching epistles, full of spiritual grace and Scriptural illustration, albeit despatched in the name of "this despised congregation," or "this despised handful of the Lord's heritage."

The dreary years of imprisonment drew tardily to a conclusion. Apart from such activities as he had been able to pursue outside, his labours within the walls had been considerable, despite the crowded and unhealthy condition of the wretched place.

Independent of the reek and stuffiness, triumphing with sturdy spirit and aspiring faith over persecuting laws and justices and gaolers, he made the debtors' section his pulpit and the felons' section his study. In the one he preached both to harassed saints and to the usual aggregation of debased humanity characteristic of a county jail; in the other, he produced books which form an important part of the world's Christian literature, for they include, to quote the full title: "Grace Abounding to the chief of Sinners, or a brief Relation of the exceeding mercy of God in Christ, to His poor Servant John Bunyan;

wherein is particularly shewed the manner of his conversion, his sight and trouble for sin, his dreadful temptations, also how he despaired of God's mercy, and how the Lord at length through Christ did deliver him from all the guilt and terror that lay upon him." Which title, however, seems to have struck him as leaving something lacking, for, when enlarging the book, he varied it, placing less emphasis on the power of temptation but more on the deliverance of God, so that it became: " a brief and faithful relation of the exceeding mercy of God in Christ to his poor servant John Bunyan; namely, in His taking him out of the dunghill, and converting him to the faith of His blessed Son, Jesus Christ. Here is also particularly showed, what sight of, and what trouble he had for sin; and also what various temptation he hath met with, and how God hath carried him through them." Statedly written " for the benefit of the tempted and dejected Christian," the book bore, as a motto, the appeal of the Psalmist: " Come and hear, all ye that fear God, and I will declare what He hath done for my soul " (Ps. lxvi. 16).

When, in March, 1672, Charles II issued the Declaration of Indulgence, suspending the execution of penal laws in regard to ecclesiastical matters, not only was he acting arbitrarily, but, as Bunyan saw well, this regal effort to broaden the base of religious liberty came of a desire, not to relieve the persecuted Gospellers, but to make easy the position and progress of the Roman Catholics.

Whatever subtlety, or whatever illegality, attached to the monarch's purposes and actions, the Declaration was at least truthful in its main confession, " by the sad experience of twelve yeares," that there had been " very little fruite of all these forceable Courses." The policy of " Yield or be exterminated " had admittedly failed. The announcement of the new order ran : " That there may be no pretence for any of our subjects to continue the illegal Meetings and Conventicles, Wee doe Declare, that Wee shall from time to time allow a sufficient number of places, as they shall be desired, in all parts of this Our Kingdome, for the use of such as doe not conforme to the Church of England, to meete and assemble in, in Order to their Public Worship and Devotion, which places shall be free and open to all persons."

Bunyan's release derived technically from a simple fact, far removed. The king, when escaping from England after the Battle of Worcester, sailed to France in a small trading vessel, the mate of which, a worthy Quaker named John Groves, carried him ashore, near Fécamp. After the lapse of many years Groves asked a favour of the king, by way of recompense; it was the discharge of just half-a-dozen out of the many Quakers immured in the jails. The king granted the request, wondering alike at its lateness and its self-denying simplicity. Other appeals followed, notably from that famous Quaker, George Whitehead. Finally, a general pardon, in keeping with the spirit of the Declaration, was extended to " Quakers and others " and Bunyan was released as one of the " others " —in direct response, however, to a petition addressed to the king, and signed by Bunyan himself, as well as other prisoners; which petition was favourably considered at a meeting of the Privy Council, May 17, 1672.

The actual date of the release remains obscure; but while we are left in doubt as to the day when the studded door swung back to give him liberty, we are at least sure of his spirit. He emerged, as he had passed in, a witness for God.

Seven years before, he had written, in answer to a comforting epistle sent him by a friend, a poem entitled *Prison Meditations*. It is somewhat in the manner of Lovelace's, *To Althea, From Prison*—a manner in which Bunyan delighted, as we note also by the "Shepherd-boy's Song," in the *Pilgrim's Progress*. Like most of Bunyan's verse, it is homely, as though Lovelace had discarded his wine-stained silk and put on worsted and a quiet spirit. But, also like Bunyan's verse, it flashes now and again with some beautiful and heavenly thought, characteristically expressed. The tinker's flowers, like those of Dorothea in the legend, came from Heaven; wherefore he sang:

> "For though men keep my outward man
>   Within their locks and bars,
> Yet by the faith of Christ I can
>   Mount higher than the stars.

> "When they do talk of banishment,
>   Of death, or such-like things,
> Then to me God sends heart's content,
>   That like a fountain springs."

VI   "*Bishop*" *Bunyan*

UPON being released from jail, Bunyan found himself in a position of importance and usefulness. His popularity as a preacher, and his influence as a conscientious Christian who had suffered much in the cause of spiritual freedom, were great. While some, driven by the winds of persecution or drawn by the warm sun rays of worldly advantage, had forsaken the church, he had been valiant for the truth.

The books he issued during his imprisonment—nine during the first six years and two in the second, were chiefly of an expository and appealing character, and afforded further demonstration of his ability and his devotion. That his literary productions grew fewer in the later years of his jail days may have arisen either from his zeal in the tagged lace industry—which probably commanded a " spot cash " payment, however small, and an immediate remittance for Mrs. Bunyan and the " poor blind one "—or from publishers' difficulties in the way of securing a licence to publish or an opportunity to sell.

That he was held in increasing regard by

the church of which he was a member, is shown by his being chosen, on January 21, 1672, and therefore while he was still a prisoner, as their pastor. The entry in the church records—which are marked by a gravity and ingenuousness which are an index of spiritual earnestness and simple faith—reads: "After much seeking God by prayer, and sober conference formerly had, the Congregation did at this meeting with joynt consent (signified by solemne lifting up of their hands) call forth and appoint our brother John Bunyan to the pastorall office or eldership. And he, accepting thereof, gave up himself to serve Christ and His Church in that charge; and received of the elders the right hand of fellowship."

This appointment did not postulate a forsaking of his old trade; he was still John Bunyan, the brasier or tinker. His licence under the Declaration was "to bee a Teacher of the Congregation allowed by Us in the howse of Josias Roughed, Bedford, for the use of such as doe not conforme to the Church of England, who are of the Perswasion commonly called Congregationall. With further licence and permission to him the said John Bunyon to teach in any other place licensed by Us according to our said Declaration." The licence was signed by Arlington.

With the energy of zeal and faith, Bunyan took full and immediate advantage of his opportunity. Roughead, whose house was specified in the licence, was a member of Bunyan's congregation, and had himself suffered much in the times of persecution. He conveyed his barn, with the orchard in which it stood, to " John Bunyan of the Towne of Bedford, Brasier," and five others, as representatives of the church, for a sum of £50. On this site, the church, of which Gifford, Burton, and Bunyan were the first three pastors, still finds its home.

At no time in Bunyan's career were his vigour of mind, decision of character, and promptness of action more strongly evidenced than at this crisis. When applying for his licence to preach, and also for the licence for the barn, he likewise put in an application for further licences for twenty-five preachers and thirty buildings—barns and private dwelling-houses—in Bedfordshire and the adjoining counties.

A man of less ardent spirit might possibly have settled down quietly to a plain round of local pastoral and preaching duty, and the simple pleasures of long-lost domesticity. It was not so with Bunyan. Bedford remained his chief centre, but he preached and evangelised far and near, until a new and holy interest in the Redeemer's Kingdom was aroused, and crowds of the ungodly flocked to hear the Good News. The care of numerous Christian causes was more or less upon him ; he was for practical purposes a sort of

Nonconformist Bishop. In fact he was jeeringly called " Bishop " Bunyan, by some of his enemies ; but they spoke more accurately than they knew.

It is not to be thought, however, that his spirit was one of rivalry with the Church of England. Nor did he for a moment seek revenge for the persecution to which he had been subjected. He simply went about his Master's business. For the principles of Christian liberty in defence of which he had suffered so much, he still stood unfalteringly. But he looked with mildness and forbearance upon men like Foster, who persistently regarded Bunyan himself and such churches as that which met in Roughead's barn as pests, to be put down, if not with legal authority, then with social scorn and superior exclusiveness.

Nevertheless, soaring above all pettiness, he stood fundamentally for Christian peace and concord. For example, in defending the position of Open Communion, he pointedly declared : "Since you would know by what name I would be distinguished from others, I tell you I would be, and hope I am, a Christian, a believer, or other such name which is approved by the Holy Ghost." The Church in the barn was defined as " Congregational," but Bunyan had the strongest objection to denominational titles, holding that " they naturally lead to divisions."

His views on Open Communion drew

vigorously expressed opposition from distinguished ministers, and he replied with the treatise entitled: *Differences about Water Baptism No Bar to Communion; or, to Communicate with Saints, as Saints, Proved Lawful*. In *A Confession of My Faith, and a Reason of My Practice in Worship*, he states: " Touching shadowish or figurative ordinances, I believe that Christ hath ordained but two in His Church, namely, Water Baptism and the Supper of the Lord: both which are of excellent use to the Church in this world; they being to us representations of the Death and Resurrection of Christ; and are, as God shall make them, helps to our faith therein. But I count them not the fundamentals of our Christianity, nor grounds or rule to communion with saints: servants they are, and our mystical ministers, to teach and instruct us in the most weighty matters of the Kingdom of God: I therefore here declare my reverent esteem of them; yet dare not remove them, as some do, from the place and end, where by God they are set and appointed; nor ascribe unto them more than they were ordered to have in their first and primitive institution. It is possible to commit idolatry even with God's own appointments. I dare have communion, church communion, with those that are visible saints by calling: with those that, by the word of the Gospel, have been brought over to faith and holiness."

The holding of strong opinions regarding Christian unity did not imply any tendency either towards latitudinarianism or looseness of administration. His great purpose was the upbuilding of the Kingdom of God; and the church records demonstrate his thorough faithfulness. For example, we have a letter written on behalf of the church to " our dearly beloved Sister Tilney "—a lady who, after enduring keen persecution, including the seizing of her entire household belongings, for declining to attend the parish church, desired to remove to London, and was now requesting her dismission to a church of which her son-in-law was pastor.

Such a letter might easily have been granted to such a suffering saint, and that without question; but Bunyan, while acknowledging the " holy and quiet behaviour with which, in the gentleness of Christ, she had suffered herself to be robbed," could not formally part with her except to a church of the satisfactoriness of which, not in details but in essentials, he was satisfied. Wherefore, in an appealing epistle, which is a model of skill and kindness in pastoral correspondence, and which illustrates Bunyan's truly spiritual concern for the flock, Sister Tilney is aptly reminded that: " For our safety and your profit, it is behooffull that we commit you to such, to be fed and governed in the Word and Doctrine, as, we are sufficiently persuaded, shall be able to deliver you up with joy at the Coming of our Lord Jesus Christ with all His saints : otherwise we (that we say not you) shall receive blushing and shame before Him and you ; yea, and you also, our honoured sister, may justly charge us with want of love, and a due respect for your eternal condition, if, for want of care and circumspection herein, we should commit you to any from whom you should receive damage, or by whom you should not be succoured and fed with the sincere milk of the incorruptible Word of God. Wherefore we may not, neither dare give our consent that you feed and fold with such whose principles and practices, in matters of faith and worship, we, as yet, are strangers to, and have not received commendations concerning, either from works of theirs or epistles of others. Yourself, indeed, hath declared that you are satisfied therein ; but, elect sister, seeing the act of delivering you up is an act of ours and not yours, it is convenient, yea, very expedient, that we, as to so weighty a matter, be well persuaded before. Wherefore we beseech you, that, for the love of our Lord Jesus Christ, you give us leave to inform ourselves yet better before we grant your request ; and that you also forbear to sit down at the table with any without the consent of your brethren."

Sister Tilney, while thus assured of the lively interest of the church, is also furnished with specific suggestions : " For the more quick expedition of this matter, we will propound before you our further thoughts: (1) Either we shall consent to your sitting down with Brother Cockain, Brother Griffith, Brother Palmer, or other, who, of long continuance in the city, have showed forth their faith, their worship, and good conversation with the Word. (2) Or if you can get a commendatory epistle from Brother Owen, Brother Cockain, Brother Palmer, or Brother Griffith, concerning the faith and principles of the person and people you mention, with desire to be guided and governed by, you shall see our readiness, in the fear of God, to commit you to the doctrine and care of that congregation. Choose you whether of these you will consent unto, and let us hear of your resolution. And we beseech you, for love's sake, you show, with meekness, your fear and reverence of Christ's institution ; your love to the congregation, and regard to your future good. Finally, we commit you to the Lord, and the Word of His grace, who is able to build you up, and to give you an inheritance among them that are sanctified. To God, the Only wise, be glory and power everlasting. Amen."

Bunyan had not spent long years in the school of suffering, and the study of the Word, without learning to use his great intellectual powers and spiritual sympathy with the tried and anxious in the high duty of imparting counsel and guidance ; many an entry in the church book proves with what zeal and ability he spent himself in the ministry ; and amid his ardent labours for the saints there shone a glorious passion to win the ungodly for Christ—even the rabble of tavern parlours and the riff-raff of fair-days.

These activities were not to continue. Another revolutionary change in his life was imminent. The people and the Prerogative were once again in collision. The current of antagonism to the Cabal, which now set in, was of irresistible strength. The city of London was horrified at the financial dishonesty of the government. No money could be raised. It therefore became necessary, in 1673, to reassemble Parliament, which had not met for nearly two years.

An effort was soon made to secure the revocation of the Declaration of Indulgence—an instrument of liberty which, for widely different reasons, was obnoxious to all parties and sects except the Roman Catholics. Macaulay, with a characteristic side-hit at the Puritans, says : " The zealous Churchman exclaimed against the favour which had been shown both to the Papist and the Puritan. The Puritan, though he might rejoice in the suspension of the persecution by which he had been harassed, felt little gratitude for a toleration which he was to share with Antichrist." This however was only a narrow view of the Puritan position ; the case was more truly put by a Nonconformist member who protested, in the course of debate: " I had much rather see the Dissenters suffer by the rigour of the law, though I suffer with them, than see all the laws of England trampled under the foot of the Prerogative, as in this example."

Shaftesbury deserted the Cabal, and from his place in the House of Lords, denounced the Indulgence as illegal. The king saw that the struggle was hopeless, and himself tore the seal from the Declaration. The floodgates of persecution were opened once more. The licences were withdrawn. The members of the Country Party were anxiously ready to support Danby—who, in his attitude to preachers of the Bunyan order, was simply a cloth-bound edition of Clarendon, unrevised. Now came a new and unsurpassed opportunity for fiery officials like Foster to hunt down praying peasants; now came in the golden prime of the spy and the common informer. Warrants multiplied by the thousand. The doors of meeting-houses were barred by constables. England was again swept by a torrent of oppression.

Bunyan, as a protagonist of the cause of religious freedom, would be an early and easy prey. No difficulty would be experienced in securing a conviction against so active and bold a preacher. The most obtuse of constables, the most cowardly of hedge-haunting informers, could readily follow a quarry whose course was open and undisguised, palpable to all. Moreover, men knew well that he would not cease for a moment on account of changes in the law, but would be found in his familiar places, in a farmhouse or churchyard, or in his own little dwelling, teaching from the Bible, praying with seeking souls, or preaching upon the eternal truths that no laws could ever suppress—redeeming love and the unsearchable riches of Christ.

Before long, the inevitable warrant was issued for his arrest. This interesting document is still in existence; it bears the signatures of no fewer than thirteen magistrates, one of them being Bunyan's fierce enemy, Foster, who had now become Chancellor of the Bishop of Lincoln, the Diocesan, and Commissary of the Court of the Archdeacon of Bedford. Of the other magistrates, it is noteworthy that at least three, Sir John Napier, Sir William Beecher and Sir George Blundell, must have known Bunyan well, for they were included in the bench which, with Kelynge as Chairman, first sentenced the tinker, in 1661.

The offence was the familiar one of preaching at Conventicles; the warrant reads:

To the Constables of Bedford and to every of them

	Whereas information and complaint is made unto us that (notwithstanding the Kings Majties late Act of most gracious generall and free pardon to all his subjects for past misdemeanours that by his said
J Napier	

clemencie and indulgent grace and favor they might be mooved and induced for the time to come more carefully to observe his Highenes lawes and Statutes and to continue in theire loyall and due obedience to his Majtie) Yett one John Bunnyon of youre said Towne Tynker hath divers times within one month last past in contempt of his Majtie's good Lawes preached or teached at a Conventicle Meeting or Assembly under color or ptence of exercise of Religion in other manner than according to the Liturgie or practiss of the Church of England These are therefore in his Majties name to comand you forthwith to apprehend and bring the Body of the said John Bunnion before us or any of us or other his Majties Justice of Peace within the said County to answer the premisses and further to doo and receave as to Lawe and Justice shall appertaine and hereof you are not to faile. Given under our handes and seales this ffourth day of March in the seven and twentieth yeare of the Raigne of our most gracious Soveraigne Lord King Charles the Second A° que D$\overline{\text{ni}}$ juxta &c 1674

W Beecher

G. Blundell

Hum: Monoux

Will ffranklin

John Ventris

Will Spencer
Will Gery   St Jo Chernocke   Wm Daniels
T Browne   W ffoster
Gaius Squire

VII The "Den"; and the Bridgeless River

THE Royal Proclamation withdrawing the preaching licences was signed on February 3, 1674, and the warrant, dated March 4, speaks of Conventicle Meetings held within "one month past"; the watch upon Bunyan's movements must therefore have been set early, and maintained with keenness. No particulars of the court proceedings have been discovered. Dr. Brown suggests that the prisoner was probably committed for trial, and held to bail, the trial taking place in due course at the Quarter Sessions following.

The place of imprisonment, almost certainly, was not the county jail, but a small building which stood midway upon the bridge over the Ouse, and which was used partly as tollhouse and partly as military store. Canon Venables rejects the theory, but Dr. Brown's array of circumstantial evidence seems convincing, especially as it is upheld by the strongest and most persistent tradition.

The warrant was indeed signed by county justices; and we should therefore naturally conclude that Bunyan was taken, in the ordinary course, to the county jail, as before. After all, however, what we are concerned to ascertain is, not simply the customary and proper procedure, but the actual facts. There were weighty reasons against following the usual method. In the county jail, Bunyan would again be, as on previous occasions, the acknowledged and recognised leader of the prisoners. Moreover, since his last release, his position as a public man had become greatly enhanced. Although in the warrant he was once again described as " tinker," he was nevertheless " Bishop " Bunyan, and he stood out in general estimation, not only as the most notable champion of religious freedom in the eastern midlands, but as one of the most distinguished Nonconformists in the country. To place such a man where he could still support, encourage, and inspire a crowd of conventicle folk was to give new life to the cause of the persecuted, as Foster and the rest of the justices knew full well.

The position of the party of intolerance was once more tremendously strong. After being galled by the State recognition of conventicles, they had now won a revolutionary victory, even over the king himself. Then, by the passing of the Test Act, the Duke of York, heir-presumptive to the throne, and a Roman Catholic, had been forced to vacate the office of Lord High Admiral. A party of such strength, as keen against conventicle preachers as against the Pope, could have little hesitation in consigning a popular and doughty preacher, honoured in Cromwell's "home counties," and "suspect" by stolid justices as being a staunch champion of religious liberty, to some place of confinement where he would be shut away from encouraging and inspiring the party of which he was so conspicuous a leader.

For such a purpose, the town jail on the bridge was exactly suitable. It is also indisputable that in May, 1675, the Town Council suddenly decided that this jail, which had lain dismantled for several years, after being partially ruined by a great flood, should be rebuilt forthwith, out of the old materials. This fits in precisely with Dr. Brown's strenuous contention; the rebuilt jail was probably the place of Bunyan's imprisonment, during the later months of 1675.

To use a gatehouse as a prison was of course a common practice. Mediæval town defences, with their massive gates, were naturally found peculiarly suitable for the purpose. The formidable West Gate of Canterbury is a conspicuous example. It was also in a gatehouse, that of the Westminster precincts, that Raleigh was confined, immediately before his execution. But Bunyan's prison was by no means an impressive-looking building. It rather suggested a combination of a street "Bar" and a strong barn or storehouse.

The bridge itself was less than five yards wide, and although a portion of the jail protruded a little upon the foundation afforded by a small island, it was at best a cramped and miserable place. Bunyan's own opinion of his new prison is shown by the significant name he gave it in the *Pilgrim's Progress*—" a den "; which appellation he never used regarding the wretched but less lonely scene of his previous incarcerations.

But no " den " could hold in check that gallant and faithful spirit or blight that brilliant and aspiring imagination. Persevering application had enriched his mind with a wide and comprehensive knowledge of men and books; and his unfailing devotion to the Bible had increasingly furnished him with Scriptural illustrations and parallels that were kept ready to hand in the treasure chest of a retentive memory. He was equipped for the work of instruction and consolation to which God had called him apart, even into the " den."

Many a grim joke at the expense of the preaching tinker would pass with the wine at the tables of the world's great ones; but by the grace of God the grey walls opened out in a splendid vision of spiritual quest and Divine deliverance, and so it came that to the rattling of the corn-carts under the archway, the lapping of the stream among the weeds, or the moaning of the winter wind, this solitary child of stress and sorrow began with glowing heart, the great book which renders his name intimately fragrant and precious even amid the mighty company of the immortals of English literature.

Eventually, a release was secured, through an order obtained from the Lord Chancellor, and operative through Thomas Barlow—Bishop of Lincoln—whose good offices had also been sought in a letter addressed to him by the famous Dr. John Owen, formerly chaplain to Cromwell, and who was still, in his mature years, one of the most generally respected of Nonconformists; Bunyan himself spoke of him as "that mighty armour-bearer."

Barlow (as Canon Venables remarks) was somewhat of a time-server, but he was not unwilling, while chary of taking risks, to oblige Owen, whose tutor he had been at Oxford. Again the facts are somewhat obscure, but the fact of the release, after an imprisonment of six months, is admitted. Thus set free for the third time, Bunyan immediately resumed his preaching and pastoral duties; he was once more the "Bishop."

Despite the stormy condition of politics, he was henceforward left unmolested. The views and instructions of Barlow would doubtless have their silencing effect upon such leading persecutors as Foster. The character of Bunyan's writings, too, must have demonstrated that, polemical as he could be upon occasion, his aims were first of all spiritual, and that the Government need not in the least fear any Rye House Plot among the simple-minded Bedford fellowship of believers: a revolution was assuredly sought, but it was in the hearts of men, and to be wrought, not with carnal weapons, but by the power of God and with the Sword of the Spirit.

The publication of the First Part of the *Pilgrim's Progress*, in 1678, won for Bunyan an instant reputation, both at home and abroad, particularly among Christians of the middle and poorer classes. In Great Britain, three editions were called for within the year. The New England Colonies were as enthusiastic as the mother country. Holland and France speedily had translations. It was a book for all the world.

Meantime, his reputation as a preacher had spread even among the frivolous company who dallied with the dice in the galleries of Whitehall, or followed in the king's train by the banks of the Canal. According to an old story, Charles once asked Owen: "How can a man of your erudition sit to hear an illiterate tinker prate?" The anecdote has perhaps become a little dilapidated in transmission. Charles' large common sense certainly enabled him to appraise the value of natural ability; but although the remark scarcely confirms Rochester's view that the king "never said a foolish thing," Owen's reply, as reported, is sufficiently characteristic.

The "Den"; and the Bridgeless River 127

"Please your Majesty," said the great divine, "I would gladly give all my learning for the tinker's power of preaching."

It is very possible that Owen assured Charles, or Danby, not simply of Bunyan's sincerity, which would be a small matter to them, but of his freedom from any intent to conspire. In any case, Bunyan appears to have been left to preach much as he pleased, during the remainder of the reign.

Although pastoral duty necessitated his being chiefly in Bedford, or at any rate in his "bishopric," Bunyan yet paid occasional visits to London, to see his publishers and to preach. Numerous leading Nonconformists held him in high esteem, and important congregations—such as that of Pinners' Hall, Old Broad Street—delighted to welcome him. His preaching to Owen's flock at Moorfields brought him into touch with Fleetwood and Desborough, and with Sir John Hartop and other church members of distinction.

Nevertheless, although some of his biographers very naturally chronicle his association with conspicuous people, there is nothing to show that his view of life narrowed for a moment from that splendid outlook which saw in all men potential or actual witnesses for Christ, irrespective of position or title. Mingling with the great was to him no more than mingling with the poor: "Are ye not all brethren?" He remained unspoilt, a godly man marked by simplicity of life and modesty of bearing; still the ambassador of Christ, the pilgrim of God.

In the course of his journeys in the Gospel, he would be asked by friends to accept this or that little token of remembrance—such a slight gift as might be given or pressed upon him on the occasion of an anniversary day or a special visit—a small cabinet, or a malacca-cane "pilgrim's staff." Even so simple a matter has been distorted by the critical sourness of a later generation, to mean that the pilgrim "collected rare and valuable pieces of old furniture and plate." Probably he never gave these three or four simple gifts a thought, except as being expressions of the goodwill of fellow-pilgrims. The silver mines of Demas possessed no attraction for him, as his whole life testifies. How ardently his spirit hated the idea of making personal profit out of the Kingdom of God appeared in his reply to a well-intentioned friend, who offered to accept the preacher's son as an apprentice, without any premium. "God," said Bunyan, "has not sent me to advance my family, but to preach the Gospel." The author of that retort was more than a collector of curios.

During the remaining years of his life, his dwelling-place, in St. Cuthbert Street, Bedford, not far from the meeting-house, was a small double-fronted cottage, having a steeply sloping, old-fashioned red-tile roof; there were three rooms on the ground floor, and above was a garret, with a dormer window. It is interesting to have the testimony, regarding the simplicity of the little house, of a stranger who made a pilgrimage thither during Bunyan's lifetime, with the intention of "seeing the study" of so famous an author and preacher; he found the "study" to be the plainest of apartments; the literary equipment consisted of the Bible, with a copy or two of some of Bunyan's own works.

The whole aspect of the cottage showed that it was the dwelling of a person in very humble circumstances. A minister who visited it in 1774 said it was then let for about forty shillings per annum; on which record Offor commented, in 1847; "Allowing for the difference in the value of money, it would have now let for about £5 or £6 a year. How humble an abode for so great a benefactor to the world!"

Upon James II succeeding to the throne, there was obviously a likelihood of a re-arrest of Bunyan, particularly in the days following Monmouth's rebellion and Sedgmoor fight. But then, again, royal favour veered round towards toleration, although James, like Charles, looked upon the granting of religious liberty, not as a good in itself, but solely as a means of strengthening Roman Catholicism.

One of Bunyan's last stands for righteousness and truth was in this connection, against the endeavours of James to bribe the

Nonconformists, by a new Declaration of Indulgence, into an acceptance of despotic and unconstitutional rule. Penal laws against Nonconformists were suspended, and it was forbidden to molest any religious assembly. Which is to say, Nonconformists might meet to worship God, without becoming liable to imprisonment or the confiscation of their goods.

The Declaration of the previous reign had been pronounced illegal by Parliament; it had been withdrawn, in however ungracious a fashion, by the king. Yet, James was not daunted by the memory of his brother's failure, from making this fresh effort to further the cause of the Scarlet Woman. He too had an attractive and plausible case. That Nonconformists should enjoy the right to assemble together in worship was a matter of elementary justice. Parliament, however, refused to grant it, and the Established Church opposed it; yet it was graciously proffered by the royal hand. Should those who had struggled so long and endured so much for religious liberty at length reject it, simply because it was come from the palace instead of the Parliament House? The temptation was a very real one.

Nonconformity, however, resisted and rejected the specious offer, choosing rather to suffer affliction than to purchase freedom by the sacrifice of principle. Baxter was released from prison; Howe was allowed to return from banishment; but they were one with

The " Den " ; and the Bridgeless River 131

the rest of the Presbyterian body in standing by the Constitution. Kiffin was sent for by the king, who intimated to the veteran Baptist that he was to be made an Alderman of the city of London ; but Kiffin and the Baptists were as steadfast as the Presbyterians.

Baxter, Howe and Kiffin were great and honoured leaders, but there was one other whose power and reputation among the common people were so great that he could by no means be overlooked—the ex-prisoner of Bedford jails. Bunyan was accordingly approached. A messenger of the court, probably the Earl of Ailesbury, intimated that he might be appointed to a place under the Government. Three members of his congregation were appointed, by an Order in Council, to be members of the Town Council of Bedford. But the temptations of ease and profit could not win over the man of God to the powers of this world. He declined to receive Ailesbury, or to accept any favours whatsoever.

While political events ripened swiftly to the day of Revolution, Bunyan was still occupied with the work of God. The royal recognition of the Nonconformists held back the forces of persecution ; Barlow, too, was still at Lincoln ; and Foster was eager to do the king's will in any event. But whether authorities smiled or frowned or merely looked wearily in another direction, John Bunyan, soul-winner and brasier, yet preached the Good News of sins forgiven. All England seemed to be singing *Lillibullero;* but, while as zealous as any in desiring the confusion of Popery, his song was rather of the joy of the Lord, the casting out of that old serpent the devil, and the proclamation of the great deliverer of the soul, Immanuel.

The manner of his passing was pathetic. The pilgrim died on a pilgrimage of peace, for his end came while away from home, on a journey undertaken for the express purpose of reconciling an estranged father and son. The embassy proved successful; but Bunyan returned no more to the banks of the Ouse.

In the course of his pastoral career, he had won a noble reputation for peace-making; the beautiful task was one in which he delighted. Wherefore, when the young man concerned sought out the cottage in St. Cuthbert's Street, and implored mediatorial aid, there could be but one answer forthcoming. Bunyan set out on horseback for Reading where the father lived, and where he himself had often preached. His pleasurable duty fulfilled, he bade farewell to father and son, and proceeded, not directly homeward, but towards London, for he had carried with him from Bedford the manuscript of a book entitled: *The Acceptable Sacrifice; or, The Excellency of a Broken Heart,* which he was proposing to publish.

Travelling was slow; even the best roads were exceedingly poor. Pepys has related how, travelling in his own coach, he lost his way on the Newbury road, west of Reading. Bunyan's long ride was rendered additionally trying by a heavy rainstorm, but he struggled on. His goal was a grocer's shop, kept by one of his particular friends, John Strudwick, at the sign of the Star, on Snow Hill. Past Tyburn and so along Holborn to the bridge over the Fleet, he urged his way, weary, soaked with rain and severely chilled.

Strudwick, a genial and godly man, and a member of the congregation of George Cockayn, who also had long held Bunyan in high esteem, would warmly greet his welcome visitor. The ensuing few days seem to have been devoted to resting and to the publishing matter of *The Acceptable Sacrifice*. Immediately his presence in London became known, too, he would inevitably receive numerous requests to preach, for an intimation that he would occupy the pulpit sufficed to draw a vast assembly, and ministers loved him for his faithfulness and sincerity, no less than they honoured him for his abilities.

Once only he seems to have preached; it was at Gamman's Meeting-house "near Whitechapel." His text was John i. 13, and his concluding words, according to a report subsequently published, were: "Consider that the holy God is your Father, and let this oblige you to live like the children of God, that you may look your Father in the face, with comfort, another day."

The sermon was preached on Sunday, August 19, 1688. On the following Tuesday a violent fever seized him. He was now in his sixtieth year, and his weary frame, exhausted by hardship and exposure, and also by incessant labour, in season and out of season, could no longer withstand a severe illness.

For ten days he lay battling with the fever, and striving to overcome the fatal weakness which gradually crept over him. Whether his wife and children were with him, no record tells; but we may be reasonably certain that in his quiet chamber his thoughts would go back to her loyal championship of him in the upper guest-room at the Swan, before the angry squires and justices.

To send word to Bedford would take two days; the journey to London would occupy two more. Perhaps when the urgent symptoms appeared the time was too short and the message, if one was sent, arrived too late. But Cockayn, the godly pastor of Redcross Street, would certainly be by his bedside, and Strudwick himself, when the horn of the heavenly post sounded, amid the traffic and jostle of Snow Hill, with the Summons Home for John Bunyan. Above all, there was the Presence which had been with him since the day when first he saw, as with the eyes of his soul, Jesus Christ, his righteousness, at God's Right Hand. It is impossible to part Bunyan dying from Bunyan living;

upon the Friend of his lonely prison days, who had piloted him safely through all the storm-tossed course of his life, he would rest also in the end.

The ready pens of friends took down some of the weighty truths and holy counsels which he uttered in the intervals of his illness. Life gradually ebbed away. But it was with the praises of God upon his failing lips that he came at length to the margin of the bridgeless river, the crossing of which by humble pilgrims he had himself imagined with such sublimity and pathos.

It is no pining lament but a hymn of victory, albeit sung with tears, that we seem to catch from the little group in that peaceful death-chamber, over the grocer's shop by the muddy Fleet. To join that kind company would have been to find ourselves in an atmosphere of consecration and prayer, and, above all, of triumph in Christ. Only with the unfaltering, though tender and loving farewell suitable to the departure of a scarred warrior whose trust no waters could quench— a farewell that, echoing midway across the river, might then be lost in the shout from the other shore—could leave be taken of one whose lovely picture of the vanquishing of death is itself deathless.

One of the most touching passages in the *Pilgrim's Progress* might almost be taken as a description of the final scenes around Bunyan's deathbed. Mr. Standfast, after receiving the summons to "prepare for a change of life," found " a great calm at that time in the river," and as he made his way through, was able to have sweet conversation with his waiting friends, saying : " This river has been a terror to many ; yea, thoughts of it have often frightened me ; but now methinks I stand easy ; my foot is fixed upon that, upon which the feet of the priests that bare the Ark of the Covenant stood, while Israel went over this Jordan. The waters indeed are to the palate bitter, and to the stomach cold ; yet the thoughts of what I am going to, and of the conduct that waits for me at the other side, doth lie as a glowing coal at my heart. I see myself now at the end of my journey ; my toilsome days are ended. I am going now to see that Head that was crowned with thorns, and that Face that was spit upon, for me. I have formerly lived by hearsay and faith ; but now I go where I shall live by sight, and shall be with Him in whose company I delight myself." Thus talked Mr. Standfast, of the band of shadowy pilgrims who are yet so real ; thus talked Bunyan.

It is part of the story of Mr. Standfast that " while he was thus in discourse his countenance changed," and that he was ceased to be seen of his friends after they heard him say : " Take me, for I come to Thee ! " Froude mistakenly gives this cry of Mr. Standfast as being Bunyan's own saying ; naturally, it

The "Den"; and the Bridgeless River

was very characteristic of what he actually did say, some account of which survives, in *A Continuation of Mr. Bunyan's Life*, appended to *Grace Abounding*, and doubtless written by George Cockayn, as a comparison of the style with that of Cockayn's signed preface to *The Acceptable Sacrifice*, seems clearly to show.

From that sketch we learn that Bunyan bore his illness " with much constancy and patience, and expressed himself as if he desired nothing more than to be dissolved, and to be with Christ, in that case esteeming death as gain, and life only a tedious delaying of felicity expected; and finding his vital strength decay, having settled his mind and affairs as well as the shortness of his time and the violence of his disease would admit, with a constant and Christian patience he resigned his soul into the hands of his most merciful Redeemer, following his Pilgrim from the City of Destruction to the New Jerusalem; his better part having been all along there, in holy contemplation, pantings, and breathings after the hidden manna and water of life—as by many holy and humble consolations expressed in his letters to several persons in prison and out of prison."

The tiny book entitled: *Mr. John Bunyan's Dying Sayings*, a collection of aphorisms, gathered perhaps by Cockayn, and classified under appropriate headings, demonstrates that the great themes which were the staple of his conversation in life dominated and illuminated his thoughts even to the end. Of Sin, he said, for example: "If sin be so dreadful a thing as to wring the heart of the Son of God, how shall a poor wretched sinner be able to bear it?" Of Affliction: "Did we heartily renounce the pleasures of the world, we should be very little troubled as to our afflictions; that which renders an afflicted state so insupportable to many is, that they are too much addicted to the pleasures of this life, and so cannot endure that which makes a separation between them." Of Repentance: "Repentance carries with it a divine rhetoric, and persuades Christ to forgive multitudes of sins committed against Him." Of Prayer: "Prayer will make a man cease from sin, or sin will entice a man to cease from prayer. The spirit of prayer is more precious than treasures of gold and silver. Pray often, for prayer is a shield to the soul, a sacrifice to God, and a scourge for Satan." Of Suffering: "It is not every suffering that makes a martyr, but suffering for the Word of God, after a right manner; that is, not only for righteousness, but for righteousness' sake; not only for truth, but out of love to truth; not only for God's Word, but according to it; to wit, in that holy, humble, meek manner, as the Word of God requireth."

Finally he said, of the Joys of Heaven: "Christ is the desire of nations, the Joy of angels, the Delight of the Father; what solace then must that soul be filled with, that hath the possession of Him to all eternity. If you would be better satisfied what the beatifical vision means, my request is, that you would live holily, and go and see."

Differing statements have been made, from time to time, regarding the precise date of Bunyan's death. The appendix to *Grace Abounding* gives August 12 (1688). In 1864 a writer in a London antiquarian magazine announced that he had come across a written copy of the inscription which formerly existed on the tomb, and that this document gave the date as the 17th. Since however the Whitechapel sermon was preached on the 19th, neither of the two dates could be correct; and, as Dr. Brown notes, it is probable that no inscription was cut until the year 1737. The grave, we must remember, was Strudwick's; in the course of the years he was himself buried there, and it is also the resting-place of nine other persons—relatives and descendants.

The most reliable authority upon the point is probably Charles Doe, who was deeply attached to Bunyan and admired him fervently. In 1691, Doe published a small book called *The Struggler*, in which he gave a brief but circumstantial sketch of Bunyan's life and also a catalogue of his writings. The title was intended to interpret Doe himself in his strenuous and appealing efforts to collect and reprint in a Standard Edition, all the literary work that Bunyan ever wrote. Both in the sketch and in a note at the foot of the catalogue, the date of the death is given as "August 31."

Again, the church records at Bedford show that September 4 was kept as a day of "prayre and humilyation for this Heavy Stroak upon us, ye Death of deare Brother Bunyan." This was the first entry referring to the event—the tidings of which, evidently, had only just been received. Other entries follow and they demonstrate the profound sorrow and surprise which the news called forth. In the two succeeding weeks, also, days of prayer were observed; of the second of these it is solemnly recorded that "the whole congregation mett to Humble themselves before God by ffasting and prayre, for His Hevy and Sevear Stroak upon us in takeing away our Honoured Brother Bunyan by death."

The date of the commencement of these memorial assemblies harmonises with Doe's unhesitating statements. August 31 is doubtless correct; and it is accepted in the inscription which is now upon the tomb. But the question as to whether this or that day was the one upon which Bunyan departed to be with Christ is after all a comparatively small matter, as related to what the man himself was and did; nor would the point be laboured but for the very proper ambition of chroniclers to be precise in all details.

Close to the spot where, near the northern boundary of the City of London, George Whitefield took his stand amid motley crowds, and thundered forth the convicting truth of God or wept over sinners, there are three famous burial grounds, each within only a few yards of the others, and yet each containing the hallowed dust of an apostolic pilgrim and spiritual warrior whose preaching and writings deeply stirred and powerfully and permanently affected, not Britain alone, but the whole world.

In one of these unadorned sanctuaries of the immortal dead lies John Wesley at the rear of the Chapel called after his name. The second is one that was formerly filled with graves whose grassy hillocks, according to the custom of the early Friends, were left without an identifying stone. By a transformation wrought in the nineteenth century the quiet place of sepulture, so weird in its appearance, was levelled, and changed into a pleasant garden—an oasis of grass and shrubs centred in a desert of dull factories and warehouses. One small headstone has been placed in the greensward; it bears the name of George Fox.

The third burial ground is that of Bunhill Fields. It is a somewhat uninviting area, enclosed by dingy walls and railings and wearing a general aspect of down-at-heel shabbiness; yet at every turn of its asphalte and gravel walks we come upon some name which shines like a star in the religious or literary annals of England; soldiers of the Parliament; preachers whose holiness and eloquence made them the pillars of spiritual religion in some of the darkest hours of our history; authors whose genius caught its interpretation in the thought of Calvary or in the sacred ideal of freedom to worship God. Here were laid Isaac Watts and Daniel Defoe; those mighty Puritans, Thomas Goodwin and John Owen; the mother of the Wesleys and Lady Ann Erskine; here, too, in some grave as yet untraced, was buried William Blake, the mystic poet and painter.

Amid these broken ranks of storm-bleached and time-wrenched tombs there is one spot to which, above all others, the children of faith, whatsoever may be the land of their birth, unfailingly make their way. It is where, in a plain brick grave, which a later generation surmounted with a memorial of excellent intention but feeble result, the Snow Hill grocer laid the precious frame, exhausted by toil and suffering, of the author of the *Pilgrim's Progress*.

VIII   The Man and his Books

FAR from being a cold and superior person, walking elusively apart from the highway of life, Bunyan was intensely human. His style breathes intimate comradeship. Nothing seems detached or icy. The impression upon the mind is that of a strong and distinctive personality, warm-hearted always ; moreover of one engaged with headlong abandonment in a tremendous and glorious conflict.

The statesmen who harassed him, the justices who sentenced him, and the dignitaries who scoffed at him as a " prating tinker," are mere suits of clothes in comparison with this man of mighty intellect, who was yet the willing bond-servant of Christ, sanctified unto Him to battle or patiently endure ; and who is also our very excellent friend.

It is inevitable that we should desire to know something of the personal appearance of such a man. Of this we learn a good deal from the still-surviving portraits, painted or sketched from life. The pencil drawing on vellum, by Robert White, preserved in the Cracherode Collection now in the British Museum, is the work of a portraitist famous in his day as an artist and engraver. The sketch was a study for the " sleeping portrait " which was published, in 1679, as the frontispiece to the third edition of the *Pilgrim's Progress*. Dr. Brown mentions of White, that his original sketches were sometimes considered superior to his finished engravings, and this criticism will probably be endorsed by those who have compared the pencil sketch of Bunyan with the "sleeping portrait" engraving. White also engraved a full-length portrait, prepared from the same pencil sketch, for the first edition of the *Holy War*. The "sleeping portrait" has been several times copied, for new editions, by new engravers, and each engraver has usually signed his plate as though it were an entirely original effort.

A bold and characteristic portrait is that by Sturt, which formed the frontispiece to the edition of Bunyan's works prepared by Charles Doe, but of which only one volume was issued—in 1692. Doe describes this portrait as being "cut in copper, from an original paint done to the life," by Bunyan's "very good friend, a limner." Who the limner was, does not appear; and the "paint" referred to by Doe has not been traced. Despite its vigour, the portrait is not altogether pleasing, and it is difficult, in this case also, to avoid the conclusion that something of the true expression has been lost in the process of engraving.

Finally, there is the oil painting, by

Thomas Sadler, purchased for the nation, in 1902, by the Trustees of the National Portrait Gallery. This picture, which dates from 1685, has been highly popular with engravers and publishers, but seems to have been somewhat difficult of access. The exquisite engraving after Sadler, was made not from the picture itself, but from " a rare print after the picture." In the course of this double transmission, the actual expression was lost; Holl's technique is altogether admirable, but the engraving is not a true portrait of Bunyan. It has been reserved for modern mechanical processes, in their special field of tributary service, to effect an exact reproduction of Sadler's painting.

The " pen portrait " which is given in the continuation to *Grace Abounding* forms a capital companion, simple and ingenuous, to the productions of artists:

" He appeared to be of a stern and rough temper; but in his conversation mild and affable, not given to loquacity or much discourse in company, unless some urgent occasion required it; observing not to boast of himself, or his parts, but rather seem low in his own eyes, and submit himself to the judgment of others; abhorring lying and swearing; being just, in all that lay in his power, to his word, not seeming to revenge injuries, loving to reconcile differences, and make friendship with all; he had a sharp quick eye, accomplished with an excellent discerning of persons, being of good judgment and quick wit."

Thus much of his manner and character. As for his personal appearance " He was tall of stature, strong-boned, though not corpulent, somewhat of a ruddy face, with sparkling eyes, wearing his hair on his upper lip, after the old English fashion ; his hair reddish, but in his latter days, time had sprinkled it with grey ; his nose well set, but not declining or bending, and his mouth moderately large ; his forehead something high, and his habit always plain and modest."

" And thus," concludes this word of honest tribute, " we have impartially described a person whose death hath been much regretted ; a person who had tried the smiles and frowns of time ; not puffed up in prosperity, nor shaken in adversity, always holding the golden mean."

Another sketch of special interest is given in the Preface contributed to Doe's edition, of 1692, by Ebenezer Chandler, who succeeded Bunyan in the Bedford pastorate, and John Wilson, of Hitchin. Both these excellent men were warm personal friends of Bunyan's. They say :

"His fancy and invention were very fertile. His wit was sharp and quick, his memory tenacious. His understanding was large and comprehensive, his judgment sound and deep in the fundamentals of the Gospel, as his writings evidence. The grace of God was magnified in him and by him, and a rich anointing of the Spirit was upon him; and yet this great saint was always in his own eyes the chiefest of sinners, and the least of saints. There was indeed in him all the parts of an accomplished man, and for his piety and sincerity towards God, it was apparent to all that conversed with him. He was not only well furnished with the helps and endowments of nature, beyond ordinary, but eminent in the graces and gifts of the Spirit, and fruits of holiness. His carriage was affable and meek to all; yet bold and courageous for Christ's and the Gospel's sake. He was much struck at in the late times of persecution, and his sufferings were great, under all which he behaved himself like Christ's soldier, being far from any sinful compliance to save himself, but did cheerfully bear the cross of Christ. His countenance was grave and sedate, and did so to the life discover the inward frame of his heart, that it was convincing to the beholders; and did strike something of awe into them that had nothing of the fear of God."

And as he was in his daily walk and general demeanour and testimony, so he was in his fulfilment of pastoral duty. Chandler and Wilson declared: "He was laborious in his work of preaching, and diligent in his preparation for it, not doing the work of the Lord negligently. He was faithful in dispensing the Word, and discharging his duty to God and man. Where he saw cause of reproof, he did not spare for outward circumstances, whether in the pulpit or no ; and as ready to administer comfort and succour the tempted ; a son of consolation to the broken-hearted and afflicted, yet a son of thunder to secure and dead sinners. His remembrance is sweet and refreshing to many, and so will continue : for ' the righteous shall be had in everlasting remembrance.' "

Bunyan's great abilities as a preacher are beyond dispute. He was a born expositor. The Bible was his constant companion, and he obtained a surprising mastery of its contents, comparing Scripture with Scripture and laying up a rich treasure of divinity and of spiritual allusion and illustration. For every occasion and every person he seemed to have exactly the fitting word, as though the books of the Bible, at the call of the Spirit, spoke in the chambers of memory, saying : " This is the phrase, this the incident, that will strike to the heart or heal the wound."

Hence, any vain and contemptuous person who anticipated " sport," or at least a speedy triumph when engaging him in argument, was disillusioned. Thus it was with a noted scholar, Professor Smith, of Cambridge, who once, at the conclusion of a sermon preached by Bunyan in a barn, in a Cambridgeshire village, demanded : " What right had you to tell the audience that you knew most of them to be unbelievers ? Did not St. Paul call the people to whom he wrote, 'saints,' and 'beloved of God?' You are uncharitable and not fit to preach."

Smith's real ground of annoyance, it afterwards transpired, was not the doctrine of the sermon, but the fact that a layman—and a tinker at that—should have the effrontery to preach the Gospel at all. Bunyan answered him aptly enough, by saying that Christ, speaking from a ship to a crowd on the shore, taught in a Parable that there were four kinds of ground into which the Good Seed fell, but only one that brought forth fruit: "then" said the tinker to the professor, "your conclusion is, that the Lord Jesus Christ Himself wanted charity, and was not fit to preach the Gospel."

The writer who, in 1700, gave a short sketch of Bunyan's life, relates a circumstantial story referring to the conversion of William Bedford, afterwards the founder of a Christian cause at Royston, a Cambridgeshire town within Bunyan's regular sphere of preaching. The incident occurred at Melbourn, where: "The people being gathered together in the churchyard, a Cambridge scholar, and none of the soberest of them either, enquired what was the meaning of that concourse of people (it being upon a week-day); and being told that one Bunyan was to preach there, he gave a boy twopence to hold his horse, saying 'he was resolved to hear the tinker prate.'"

Bedford listened to his spiritual profit, and left the churchyard a changed man; doubtless he was a type of the critical class of hearers who, drawn chiefly by curiosity to hear the tinker expound, first learned the true message and power of Christianity while mingling with the village crowds who flocked to hear the godly and convincing " prating."

It is perhaps not surprising that, amid the novel and complex circumstances of the times, many Cambridge dignitaries and students warmly detested lay preaching, but it is to the credit of the University that the brutal violence with which the undergraduates had treated the early Friends had died down. The encounters with Bunyan were simply sharp arguments. In such debates, pointed if brief, he was a formidable antagonist. His extraordinary knowledge of the Bible, and swift application of its truths, enabled him to rout his adversaries. "Fitzjames's blade was sword and shield." Or, more exactly, Bunyan was spiritually skilled in the use of the "right Jerusalem blade" of which Mr. Valiant-for-Truth says: "Let a man have one of these blades, with a hand to wield it, and skill to use it, and he may venture upon an angel with it. He need not fear its holding, if he can but tell how to lay on. Its edges will never blunt. It will cut flesh and bones, and soul and spirit, and all" (Eph. vi. 17; Heb. iv. 12).

An argument would sometimes turn upon

a simple point of common sense; and in that quality Bunyan was the equal of any critic the age could produce. Moreover he often showed, when attacked, that a plain man of ability and understanding, who was also a close student of Scripture, might possess the better scholarship, and prove the better theologian and expositor.

A University man once stopped him on the road, near Cambridge, and demanded: "How dare you preach, not having the original Scriptures?" Bunyan replied with a counter-question: "Have you yourself the original Scriptures, written by the prophets and apostles?" "No," his critic rapped out, "but I have what I know to be the true copies of those originals." "And I," retorted Bunyan, "believe the English Bible to be a true copy also." Whereat the petulant scholar suddenly tired of debate and rode away.

Bunyan's abilities were too obvious and too brilliant to be suppressed by any fine scorn of the mighty. He was "made for mankind," in the service of God. The testimony of his contemporaries in that service, whether ministers or laymen, witnessed that he was a wonderful soul-winner, and an admirable pastor; but, while his constituency was primarily typified in the congregation at Bedford Meeting, which consisted chiefly of humble work-people and tradesmen, although in the later years not without a sprinkling of people of education and influence —his gifts of lucid exposition, and more particularly of powerful and pathetic writing, were of a character calculated to arrest the attention, not simply of one section of the community, but of all.

The majority of his books were formed and shaped from sermons. We can trace his method from his *Introductory Epistle* to *The Holy City*—an exposition, in prison, of Revelation 21 and 22. To give his own words:

" The occasion of my first meddling with this matter was as followeth : Upon a certain First Day, I being together with my brethren in our prison chamber, they expected that, according to our custom, something should be spoken out of the Word for our mutual edification ; but at that time I felt myself, it being my turn to speak, so empty, spiritless, and barren, that I thought I should not have been able to speak among them so much as five words of truth, with life and evidence ; but at last it so fell out that providentially I cast mine eye upon the eleventh verse of the one-and-twentieth chapter of this prophecy ; upon which, when I had considered awhile, methought I perceived something of that jasper in whose light you there find this Holy City is said to come or descend ; wherefore having got in my eye some dim glimmerings thereof, and finding also in my heart a desire to see farther into, I with a few groans did carry my meditations to the Lord Jesus for a blessing, which He did forthwith grant according to His grace ; and, helping me to set before my brethren, we did all eat, and were well refreshed ; and behold also, that while I was in the distributing of it, it so increased in my hand that of the fragments that we left, after we had well dined, I gathered up this basketful."

As he pondered, the thought still grew upon him : " wherefore setting myself to a more narrow search, through frequent prayer to God, what first with doing, and then with undoing, and after that with doing again, I thus did finish it."

It is therefore clear that he was no careless workman but ever laboured toward perfection. The titles themselves suggest thoroughness of treatment, and spiritual enjoyment in distilling all the beauties of a subject. Thus, the full title of *The Holy City* reads : " The Holy City ; or, The New Jerusalem : wherein its goodly light, walls, gates, angels, and the manner of their standing, are expounded : also her length and breadth, together with the golden measuring-reed explained : and the glory of all unfolded. As also, the numerousness of its inhabitants : and what the tree and water of life are, by which they are sustained. ' Glorious things are spoken of thee, O city of God ' : Ps. lxxxvii. 3. ' And the name of the city from that day shall be, The Lord is there ' : Ezek. xlviii. 35."

His expository works were numerous, the

majority were intended primarily for the encouragement of Christians; their outstanding feature is the exaltation of Christ as Saviour and Advocate, and the one hope of the Israel of God. Others, again, were in the nature of Gospel appeals and warnings; for example: *Come and Welcome, to Jesus Christ*, which is packed full of Evangelical truth and argument and contains also so great a number of Scripture references and allusions as to be itself a sufficient demonstration of its author's extraordinary and ready knowledge of the Bible.

Its spirit and its appeals are evidence also that, while ministering to the saints, Bunyan did not become stagnant of soul. The text was John vi. 37. One striking passage is specially characteristic:

" God hath prepared a Mercy-seat, a Throne of grace to sit on; that thou mayest come thither to Him, and that He may from thence hear thee and receive thee. 'I will commune with thee,' saith He, 'from above the mercy-seat' (Ex. xxv. 22). As who shall say: 'Sinner, when thou comest to Me, thou shalt find Me upon the mercy-seat, where also I am found of the undone, coming sinner. Thither I bring My pardons; there I hear and receive their petitions, and accept them to My favour.'

" God hath also prepared a golden altar for thee to offer thy prayers and tears upon. It is called a 'golden' altar to show what worth it is in God's account : for this golden altar is Jesus Christ ; this altar sanctifies thy gift, and makes thy sacrifice acceptable. This altar, then, makes thy groans, golden groans ; thy tears, golden tears ; and thy prayers, golden prayers, in the eye of that God thou comest to, coming sinner (Rev. viii. 3 ; Matt. xxiii. 19 ; Heb. x. 10 ; I Pet. ii. 5).

"God hath strewed all the way, from the gate of hell, where thou wast, to the gate of heaven, whither thou art going, with flowers out of His own garden. Behold how the promises, invitations, calls, and encouragements, like lilies, lie round about thee! Take heed that thou dost not tread them under foot, sinner. With promises, did I say? Yea, He hath mixed all those with His own name ; His Son's name ; also with the name of mercy, goodness, compassion, love, pity, grace, forgiveness, pardon, and what not, that may encourage the coming sinner! . . . Well, all these things are the good hand of thy God upon thee, and they are upon thee to constrain, to provoke, and to make thee willing and able to come, that thou mightest in the end be saved."

Another remarkable book is ; *The Jerusalem Sinner Saved ; or, Good news for the vilest of men.* It has gone through many editions, and has been translated into many languages. The primary thought, founded upon the command of our Lord, " that repentance and remission of sins should be preached in His name among all nations, beginning at Jerusalem," is that the worst of sinners may be saved. The book is statedly "a help for despairing souls." The "Jerusalem sinner" is urged not to despair, but to put in his or her claim with Manasseh, and Zaccheus, and Magdalene. Some of the illustrations are very homely; and the book is in a sense a complement of *Grace Abounding*. Incidentally, we get an autobiographical touch:

"I speak by experience. I was one of these great sin-breeders. I infected all the youth of the town where I was born, with all manner of youthful vanities. The neighbours counted me so: wherefore Christ Jesus took me first; and, taking me first, the contagion was much allayed all the town over.

"When God made me sigh, they would hearken, and inquiringly say: 'What's the matter with John?' They also gave their various opinions of me; but, as I said, sin cooled, and failed as to his full career. When I went out to seek the Bread of Life, some of them would follow, and the rest be put into a muse at home. Yea, almost the town, at first, would go out to hear at the place where I got good; yea, young and old for a while had some reformation on them; also some of them, perceiving that God had mercy upon me, came crying to Him for mercy too."

Yet another excellent and popular little book is *The Heavenly Footman*, which founds upon the apostolic injunction : " So run, that ye may obtain " (I Cor. ix. 24)—a telling appeal to the careless. It is full of Scripture truths, expounded with spiritual insight and applied with sympathy and skill. And this may be said, indeed, of all his expository books.

The anonymous author of an early sketch of Bunyan's life, to whom reference has already been made, gives a graphic picture of Bunyan as preacher, in the County jail :

" It was by making him a visit in prison that I first saw him, and became acquainted with him ; and I must profess I could not but look upon him to be a man of an excellent spirit, zealous for his Master's honour, and cheerfully committing all his own concernments unto God's disposal.

" When I was there, there were about sixty Dissenters besides himself there, taken but a little while before at a religious meeting at Kaistoe, in the county of Bedford, besides two eminent Dissenting ministers, Mr. Wheeler and Mr. Dun, by which means the prison was very much crowded ; yet, in the midst of all that hurry which so many new-comers occasioned, I have heard Mr. Bunyan both preach and pray with that mighty spirit of faith and plerophory of Divine assistance that has made me stand and wonder."

To this may be added the complementary testimony of Charles Doe, whose friendship with Bunyan commenced much later—not until 1684–5. The honest comb-maker attended a meeting held near Bankside, and therefore quite close to his shop, which was near the Southwark end of London Bridge; and he thus relates his experiences:

"I heard that Mr. Bunyan came to London sometimes, and preached; and because of his fame, and I having read some of his books, I had a mind to hear him. And accordingly I did, at Mr. More's meeting in a private house; and his text was: 'The fear of the wicked, it shall come upon him; but the desires of the righteous shall be granted' (Prov. x. 24). But I was offended at the text because not a New Testament one. . . . But Mr. Bunyan went on, and preached so New Testament-like that he made me admire and weep for joy, and give him my affections. Methought all his sermons were adapted to my condition and had apt similitudes, being full of the love of God, and the manner of its secret working upon the soul, and of the soul under the sense of it, that I could weep for joy, most part of his sermons."

Nor was Doe's opinion singular, for he goes on to say:

"When Mr. Bunyan preached in London, if there were but one day's notice given, there would be more people come together to hear him preach, than the Meeting-house could hold. I have seen to hear him preach, by my computation, about twelve hundred at a morning lecture, by seven o'clock, on a working day in the dark winter time. I also computed about three thousand that came to hear him one Lord's Day, at London, at a town's Meeting-house, so that half were fain to go back again for want of room, and then himself was fain, at a back door, to be pulled almost over people to get upstairs to his pulpit."

Amid all this popularity, Bunyan, naturally enough, was not without opportunities to "better" himself, in a worldly sense; but, whatever were the offers he received, he declined them. "He hath refused," says Doe, "a more plentiful income, to keep his station."

Of Bunyan's literary works, apart from those which are either sermonic or controversial, four are outstanding: *Grace Abounding* (1666); *The Pilgrim's Progress* (First Part, 1678; Second Part, 1684); *The Life and Death of Mr. Badman* (1680); and *The Holy War*.

The constituency for these writings lay chiefly, as we have seen, among the humbler class of readers. It was scarcely to be expected that fashionable circles would pay much heed to the spiritual revelations and confessions of *Grace Abounding*—the work of an obscure provincial mechanic, a maker of tagged laces, a preacher at conventicles, and one of the rabble rout of undisciplined Gospellers with whom honest justices were very properly cramming the jails.

We have also to remember that, as Sir

Sidney Lee says, Bunyan had no conscious literary aim. He realised in some measure that his work had literary quality as well as spiritual aim, but he was not aspiring to be crowned with the laurels of men; that would be a paltry ambition for one who sought nothing less than the inspiration of the saints of God, and the evangelisation of the people. After all, he wrote, primarily, because the promptings of the Spirit fired his soul. He could do no other. Acts of Parliament and county justices might stop him from preaching, but at least he could use his pen. Not of necessity to deliver consciously a constructive literary message to the age, not to emulate the great writers of the day, but certainly to edify, to build up in holiness, and to declare that—to use his own words—he could through grace "rejoice, even while I stick between the teeth of the lions in the wilderness."

Alike in its strength and pathos, the language of *Grace Abounding* is that of the mother tongue of the field and the cottage. Yet the book tells of the deepest longings of the soul, and of the inward battle between good and evil which is the fact of life nearest to the heart of any man. Bunyan conceals nothing, but bares his soul and reveals his defeats, his blindness, his crushing despair, as well as his venturing upon Christ and his triumphs in the Name that is above every name.

Modern criticism bids us beware of over-estimating *Grace Abounding* as a work of experimental religion, on the ground that it is calculated in some cases to nourish morbid imaginations. It is of course true that we do not all come Bunyan's way, and equally true that the way he came into faith and trust lay through a valley like unto that of the Shadow of Death. He is specific in his confessions of dulness and unbelief. His groanings remind us of his own Mr. Fearing, described by old Honest as " one of the most troublesome of pilgrims," and by Greatheart as " lying roaring at the Slough of Despond for about a month together." But there is no play of humour. The great underlying fact is that he was under profound conviction of sin, and blindly strode this way or that, as the impulse or hope of the moment might lead him. Nowhere does Bunyan imply that his dark experiences were necessary, or his introspection to be imitated.

The self-revealing story of such a man, moreover, could not be expressed in the terms either of the polished disquisitions of learned divines, the guarded balancings of vicars of Bray, or the petty nicenesses of conventional drawing-rooms. It takes us along paths whose gloom and chilliness and tortuousness are a warning to the traveller that this is by no means God's way of light; nevertheless the story is progressive; we reach the sunshine at last. The record is vigorous with sincerity, and lustred with the truth of God. A wronged and persecuted man, dragged from his home and his children, might conceivably have devoted himself to launching polemics against the laws and the system of government which had deprived him of liberty; but Bunyan's theme was, first of all, man under the yoke of sin; the blood of the cross; the soul's triumph in God. He is above all things the pilgrim. He will have sweet communion with Emmanuel in the way. The clouds break up; the thunder dies; he comes into peace. Looking back upon the road he declares: "I can remember my fears and doubts and sad months with comfort; for they are as the head of Goliath in my hand." Yet the fulness of which that present joy was the taste, was still to come; wherefore he concluded his Preface by pointing the saints still onward, saying: "My dear children, the Milk and Honey is beyond this wilderness. God be merciful to you, and grant that you be not slothful to go in to possess the land."

The Holy War is a "campaign-panorama" of the struggle between Emmanuel the Prince and Diabolus, for the possession of Mansoul, a "fair and delicate town" which Shaddai, the first Founder and Builder, made for His own delight. Bunyan unfolds his story in a masterly way. The narrative is full of incident; and although the book as a whole suggests the careful work of a brilliant and experienced author, rather than the bubbling vitality of a heavenly inspiration, it is yet a wonderful allegory, a prose epic, suggestive of *Paradise Lost* and *Paradise Regained*.

The entry of Diabolus into Mansoul, through subtlety; the fight between Shaddai's forces and the Diabolonians for the place; and the arrival and victory of Emmanuel the Prince, are described with astonishing spirit and captivating pungency characteristically touched with spiritual wisdom. Next, through the craft of Mr. Carnal Security, Mansoul is betrayed into self-confidence and neglects the Prince; for:

"They left off their former way of visiting Him; they came not to His royal palace as afore.

"They did not regard, nor yet take notice, that He came or came not, to visit them.

"The love-feasts that had wont to be between their Prince and them, though He made them still, and called them to them, yet they neglected to come to them, or to be delighted with them.

"They waited not for His counsels, but began to be headstrong and confident in themselves, concluding that now they were strong and invincible, and that Mansoul was secure, and beyond all reach of the foe, and that her state must needs be unalterable for ever."

Emmanuel sadly returns to His Father's Court; the Diabolonians plot a counter-revolution, and an army of " about twenty thousand terrible doubters" assaults Mansoul. Emmanuel returns; and in the battle which ensues the doubters are routed. Diabolus finally organizes a supreme expedition of extermination, raising another force of doubters, but relying more particularly upon the grim troops called "bloodmen," of the province of Loath-good, "a people that have their name derived from the malignity of their nature, and from the fury that is in them to execute it upon the town of Mansoul."

The bloodmen, persecutors, who "must have blood, else they die" (Isa. lix. 7; Jer. xxii. 17), are "all rugged villains," ranged under fierce and angry captains whose names are: Cain, Nimrod, Ishmael, Esau, Saul, Absalom, Judas, and Pope. Each captain has a standard-bearer, who carries red colours and an escutcheon. The emblazonments on these shields, as we might expect, emphatically suggest Bunyan and an open Bible, rather than Garter King-at-arms or aught reminiscent of Sir David Lindsay. In each heraldic emblem there is a touch, not of the grotesque, but of spiritual solemnity. Thus, the escutcheon of Captain Cain bore "the murdering club"; and the bearings of the others were: Captain Nimrod, "the great blood-hound"; Captain Ishmael, "one mocking at Abraham's Isaac"; Captain Esau, "one privately lurking to murder Jacob"; Captain Saul, "three darts cast at harmless David"; Captain Absalom, "the son pursuing his father's blood"; Captain Judas, "thirty pieces and the halter"; and Captain Pope, "the stake, the flame, and the good man in it."

Under their General, Lord Incredulity, the Diabolonians besiege Mansoul, but are routed in a series of conflicts by the warriors of Emmanuel, conspicuous among whom are Captains Credence, Good-hope, Patience, Experience, and Self-denial. Shaddai's dominion is thus maintained, although Diabolus himself remains at large, and a few enemies still skulk within the walls of Mansoul—notably Mr. Unbelief, who is "a nimble jack; him they could never lay hold of, though they attempted it often." Mr. Wrong-thoughts-of-Christ is put into prison, where he dies of a lingering consumption. Clip-promise, too, "a notorious villain, by whose doings much of the King's coin was abused," is hanged; and the comment upon his execution is: "Some may wonder at the severity of this man's punishment; but those who are honest traders in Mansoul are sensible of the great abuse that one clipper of promises may in little time do to the town."

Such points as the survival of Unbelief are fastened upon by Froude as evidences of literary unsatisfactoriness. The struggle, he argues, is left unfinished. Mansoul is still open to attack. Since, however, the full triumph of God is not yet, Bunyan makes the allegory true to the reality. It was for "the morning without clouds" that he looked;

and if, in concluding his book, he leaves the conquest of evil incomplete, he yet foreshadows the ultimate victory, for the final words are those of Emmanuel the Prince :

"Nor must thou think always to live by sense; thou must live upon My Word. Thou must believe, O My Mansoul, when I am from thee, that yet I love thee, and bear thee upon My heart for ever.

"Remember, therefore, O My Mansoul, that thou art beloved of Me; as I have, therefore, taught thee to watch, to fight, to pray, and to make war upon My foes; so now I command thee to believe that My love is constant to thee O My Mansoul; how have I set My heart, My love, upon thee! Watch. . . . Hold fast till I come."

The allegory is on the whole delightfully fresh and vigorous. The siege warfare suggests perhaps the Leicester type, in the Civil War, rather than the calculating science of Vauban, but is full of movement. Felicitous touches of humour feather the arrows that are shot at folly, and cowardice, and worldliness; and if the characterisation is not quite so brilliant as in his chief work, that is only to say, after all, that the *Pilgrim's Progress* outshines all other allegories, even of Bunyan himself.

It may be granted that some of the names, such as "Lord Will-be-will" and "Captain Credence," sound a little bookish, and thus seem a little removed from the vivid reality of life; not quite so actual as "Mr. Greatheart," or "Mr. Talkative," or "Sir Having Greedy." Yet there are many that bear the unmistakable Bunyan touch: "Lord Covetousness," who changed his name to "Prudent-Thrifty"; Diabolus' "trusty and greatly-beloved Mr. Profane"; "Alderman False-Peace"; and the burgess, "Mr. Pitiless."

To apply microscopic criticism, and suggest that in this or that detail an exact figurative parallel is not consistently maintained, would be pedantic. The outstanding fact is that Bunyan framed an allegory of sacred truth, and employed humour as one of his chief instruments, not only without offending our sense of awe and reverence, but with a glow of exalted fervour which sometimes attains the sublime.

For such a venture in authorship Bunyan was equipped conspicuously well. To a vivid imagination and an extraordinary gift of making the pictures of his mind live before the reader, he added an experience of both warfares—the carnal and the spiritual. He had suffered narrow escapes in each; and he had "fought upon his knees," not indeed like Widdrington at Chevy Chace, but with ardent prayers. Further, his duties both as preacher and brasier took him afield among the people, where, as others of his books suggest, he must have heard many a story of battle and siege from some of the old troopers.

And he had not to look even beyond his own immediate circle of friends to see how the saints were beset by Grace-doubters and Salvation-doubters.

It was no mere religious romance that he wrote, but rather a history of the battles of God for the soul of man. Emmanuel the Prince was not just the centre figure of a waking vision, but in very truth the Blessed One who, carrying gifts for rebels, had brought deliverance also for the oppressed soul of John Bunyan himself. "Shut up the box and put away the puppets," says Thackeray's epilogue. Bunyan's characters in the *Holy War* are too real to be called puppets.

The imagery is of the rebellious heart, the yoke of sin, the grace of God:

"Who thought, that saw our prisoners go down in irons, that they would have returned in chains of gold? Yea, they that judged themselves as they went to be judged of their Judge, were by His mouth acquitted, not for that they were innocent, but of the Prince's mercy, and sent home with pipe and tabor. But is this the common custom of princes? No: this is only peculiar to Shaddai, and unto Emmanuel, His Son."

Would the convert of Elstow write upon such a subject much as great Dryden, yonder, is writing political satires in championship of oppression, and meantime grumbles at the irregular payment of his pension? No. This allegory is to its author no mere matter of literary achievement. It is to be an instrument in the terrific business of the actual Holy War.

In *The Life and Death of Mr. Badman*, Bunyan depicts the career of an ungodly wretch, an impudent profligate and trickster who lives by his wits—lives riotously, and exults in the petty triumphs of his narrow cunning. It would be libelling even the period of Charles II to suggest that a Mr. Badman was essentially the product of that particular era, since unprincipled adventurers are sufficiently common in all times. Yet we must allow that the most august circles presented, at that epoch, an example of indulgence and profanity and greed which must have proved intoxicating to all who were of the Badman lineage, and must have added point to Bunyan's book.

Charles, by closing the Exchequer, ruined many honest merchants, who had thought themselves safe in entrusting their money to an English monarch and an English government: Badman deluded his creditors with false protests of inability to pay. The middle-class reprobate of Bedfordshire, had he made the journey to London, might have seen his own drunken adventures eclipsed by the wild exploits with which Rochester provoked the hissing even of a Covent Garden mob; although it is fair to admit that he might also have been disappointed, a little later, at Rochester's conversion. He might also have gleaned fresh hints of the devious ways of darkness from Chiffinch and the other backstairs creatures of the palace; or, his appearance and purse being equal to the occasion, he might have " revelled underneath the moon " with Grammont.

While it is well to remind ourselves that the conditions were favourable to unashamed flaunting, by men who laughed at moral principle, we have not to speculate as to the genesis of the work, for Bunyan himself tells us his precise aim:

" As I was considering with myself what I had written concerning the Progress of the Pilgrim from this world to glory, and how it had been acceptable to many in this nation, it came into my mind to write—as then, of him that was going to heaven, so now, of the life and death of the ungodly, and of their travel from this world to hell. The which in this I have done, and have put it, as thou seest, under the name and title of Mr. Badman, a name very proper for such a subject."

The narrative is forcibly written, but the detailed record of a downward pilgrimage makes a repulsive story. The catalogue of ill-deeds done does indeed point a moral; but the incidents are, inevitably, not of a character to adorn a tale. The author's plan did not include the portrayal of " whatsoever things are lovely "; his avowed intention was to teach a contrasting lesson to that of the upward pilgrimage. Having painted the

Narrow Way in its beauty and attraction, he will now present the Broad in all its ugliness and horror.

The scenery is rural; the atmosphere is that of Newgate. Fielding, in the nauseous mock-heroics of "Jonathan Wild," works the same thought, although in so different a way. Bunyan writes, as always, for the glory of God. But the story of Mr. Badman is essentially a grim and forbidding one, and the realism of some of the illustrative anecdotes has a touch of the horrible. The character of the book, as the record of one who deliberately cries: "Evil, be thou my good," necessarily narrows its constituency of readers.

The story is unfolded in a sustained dialogue between Mr. Wiseman, the relater, and Mr. Attentive, an admirable listener, who also makes sagacious comments and puts leading questions. The method therefore is that of Dent's *Plain Man's Pathway to Heaven*.

Badman is depicted as a man of considerable parts, although of utter wickedness. He manages to delude a godly young woman—an orphan who has inherited money—into marrying him. Of their family we read:

"One of them loved its mother dearly, and would constantly hearken to her voice. Now that child she had the opportunity to instruct in the principles of the Christian religion, and it became a very gracious child. But that child Mr. Badman could not abide.

He would seldom afford it a pleasant word, but would scowl and frown upon it, speak churlishly and doggedly to it, and though, as to nature, it was the most feeble of the seven, yet it oftenest felt the weight of its father's fingers.

"Three of his children did directly follow his steps, and began to be as vile as, in his youth, he was himself. Two others became a kind of mongrel professors, not so bad as their father, nor so good as their mother, but were betwixt them both. They had their mother's notions and their father's actions, and were much like those that you read of in the Book of Nehemiah; these children were half of Ashdod and could not speak in the Jews' language, but according to the language of each people" (Neh. xiii. 24).

Mr. Badman's wife dies, and he is entrapped, by a woman who is his peer in wickedness, into a second marriage. They become "as poor as owlets." Finally, he is seized with various terrible diseases. "The captain of these men of death that came against him to take him away, was the consumption." Even in illness and poverty he remains hard; when good men call to see him he puts them off with excuses, and at length gives orders for them to be told that he is asleep, or so weak for want of it that he "cannot abide any noise."

The adventures and plottings of Mr. Badman might furnish subjects for a series of

Hogarthian pictures, of the "Road to Ruin" order, except that there is no retributive end or dramatic victory of virtue. Mr. Badman passes quietly away—"he died like a lamb." In bringing the story to this conclusion Bunyan thrusts at the superstition that because any Mr. Badman has "died quietly" all must necessarily be well with him in a spiritual sense.

"The opinion of the common people concerning this kind of dying is frivolous and vain. I have seen a dog and a sheep die hardly. And thus may a wicked man do, because there is an antipathy between nature and death. But even then, when death and nature are struggling for the mastery, the soul, the conscience, may be as besotted, as senseless and ignorant of its miserable state, as the block or bed on which the sick lies."

At least one piece of flippant criticism is anticipated in the Preface, in which Bunyan pointedly addresses the reader, saying:

"Let me entreat thee to forbear quirking and mocking, for that I say Mr. Badman is dead; but rather gravely enquire concerning thyself by the Word, whether thou art one of his lineage or no; for Mr. Badman has left many of his relations behind him; yea, the very world is overspread with his kindred. True, some of his relations, as he, are gone to their place and long home, but thousands of thousands are left behind. . . . The butt therefore, that this time I shoot at, is wide. I cannot but think that this shot will light upon many, since our fields are so full of this game; but how many it will kill to Mr. Badman's course, and make alive to the Pilgrim's Progress, that is not for me to determine; this secret is with the Lord our God only, and He alone knows to whom He will bless it to so good and so blessed an end."

IX The "Pilgrim's Progress"

IN the *Pilgrim's Progress* Bunyan's genius blazed out with a force and grace and wit which brooked no denial. It is a masterpiece for all time. The tinker is henceforward among the immortals of literature.

No booksellers' puffs, artful or eloquent, heralded its appearance. No gifted and influential circle of coffee-house arbiters made its charm the talk of Society. Published in humble fashion; ill-set, ill-printed, and ill-bound; it was unadvertised except by the fame of its author, among the godly of the poorer classes, as one who had suffered long years in jail as a martyr of religious liberty, and who was a mighty preacher, a fresh and fascinating writer, and above all a good man. Yet, despite all drawbacks of the times, whether social, political or technical, the book won an immediate popularity, which, although limited at first to the small cottage, the tradesman's parlour, and the farmhouse kitchen, speedily became world-wide.

We are not to think of this surprising work of genius as the sudden production of an illiterate and unprepared mechanic. It was not that he flung aside the unmended kettles, seized a pen and "dashed off" an English classic. The root of the matter certainly was that he possessed extraordinary native gifts, being, as Edmund Gosse has said: "Unconsciously a consummate artist, and a man instinct with imagination." If Pope " lisped in numbers, for the numbers came," Bunyan at least wrote always with homely wisdom and truth and logic, and with a fire not of this world. But he could no longer be set down as ignorant; his education had considerably advanced; he was now an author of tried ability and wide experience, having proved his quality in biographical narrative, in doctrinal controversy, and in Scripture exposition. Further, he had won a deep knowledge of men and affairs, and had laboured much in that service which is the highest and holiest of all.

Seventeen years before, when interviewed in prison by the Clerk of the Peace, who attempted to frighten or cajole him into submission, he had readily retorted upon his visitor, as we have seen, with a quotation from Wickliffe. That he was familiar with the poetry of George Herbert seems certain; that he was fairly intimate with Baxter's writings is more than probable, for his own controversial works suggest that he studied, or at least read, some of the theological works of the day. It might not unreasonably be surmised that he had read this or that book, upon the strength of some slight resemblance in, for example, the *Pilgrim's Progress.* Yet the surmise might not bear the strain of a close comparison.

In considering to what extent he was familiar with secular literature, we are upon delicate ground. The likeness, in manner though by no means in subject, of " Who would true valour see," in the *Pilgrim's Progress,* to " Who would ambition shun," in *As You Like It,* seems too pronounced to be accidental; yet it is possible that Bunyan may merely have heard the original sung—perhaps on Elstow green, in the old days of his youth. Another Shakesperian touch is in a line in the rhymed Preface to the *Pilgrim's Progress*— " The Author's Apology for his Book "—in which he seems to borrow the illustration of the " jewel in the toad's head," also from *As You Like It;* but this figure is likewise used in the *Euphues* of John Lyly; hence it would be easy to digress into a speculation as to whether Bunyan had noted at any rate—and there would be little else serviceable to such a reader—the Evangelical dialogue between Euphues and Atheos.

It is however neither necessary nor safe to theorise regarding the extent of Bunyan's reading. The subject is interesting, but the evidences are extremely slender. We are untrue to the memory of the man of God if we allow ourselves to spin fancies as to whether he was acquainted with books, most of which he would himself have regarded as being essentially of this present world, and far removed from his own ideals and purposes. A touch as of Ithuriel's spear seems to recall us to the simplicities of Bunyan's life ; and we recognsie that only Mr. Worldly Wiseman would rummage among the bookshelves to show, ultimately, that in some way or another the ethereal was indebted to the mundane.

He set small store upon literature, as such. He was quick to grasp such education as would equip him for his life's work in the service of God, and which was convenient of acquirement amidst the activities of a spiritual warrior ; but when we seek for traces of formative influences, we are continually thrust back to the great fact of his assiduous devotion to the Bible—where alone he found his true " realms of gold "—and are met by such vigorous words as those of the Preface to the *Holy City*:

" The reason why you find me empty of the language of the learned, I mean their sentences and words, which others use, is because I have them not, nor have read them ; had it not been for the Bible, I had not only not done it thus, but not at all."

His reference here is specifically to " the learned fathers." Presumably, from the nature of his subject, he had Augustine chiefly in mind. But he goes on to say, in a wider sense :

"I do find in most such a spirit of idolatry concerning the learning of this world, and wisdom of the flesh, and God's glory so much stained and diminished thereby; that had I all their aid and assistance at command, I durst not make use of aught thereof. . . . I honour the godly as Christians, but I prefer the Bible before them; and having that still with me, I count myself far better furnished than if I had without it all the libraries of the two Universities. Besides, I am for drinking water out of my own cistern; that which God makes mine by the evidence of His Word and Spirit, that I dare make bold with."

The development of his style is therefore very little related to literary study in the ordinary sense. Moreover it is necessary to remember, in this connection, his statement in the Preface to *Grace Abounding*:

"I could have stepped into a style much higher than this in which I have here discoursed, and could have adorned all things more than I have here seemed to do; but I dare not. God did not play in convincing of me; the devil did not play in tempting of me; neither did I play when I sank as into a bottomless pit, when the pangs of hell caught hold upon me; wherefore I may not play in my relating of them, but be plain and simple, and lay down the thing as it was. He that liketh it, let him receive it; and he that does not, let him produce a better."

Bunyan's English is Bible English, touched with workaday English, which itself owed much to the Bible. To a sweet familiarity with the English translation, he added a splendid faculty of moulding and using the homespun talk of the common people. The Bible was his perennial source of inspiration. Much more than a record, however revealing; or a system of doctrine, however complete, the Book was food to his soul, and fire to his imagination. No human document could compare in interest or beauty with the transcendent theme of Deity tabernacling in flesh. He gained, in communion and prayer, that Divine knowledge of which the apostle declared: "Ye need not that any man teach you"; and brought forth "things old and new" from the treasure-house of the Word.

It was not of set plan that he commenced his great book. The rhymed Preface, with its "artless wood-notes wild," shows that he was occupied with another purpose altogether when the idea of the Pilgrim occurred to him:

> "And thus it was: I writing of the way
> And race of saints, in this our Gospel-day,
> Fell suddenly into an allegory
> About their journey, and the way to glory."

The thought grew; fresh ideas came to him; new thoughts as to incident and dialogue; at length—the heavenly thought was a book. He wrote, not for posterity, but in sheer enjoyment ; not with the unhesitating speed of Goldsmith, penning the *Vicar of Wakefield* to escape the bailiff and the jail, but in odd moments of time within jail doors. This indeed suited admirably well with his custom of embroidering, and polishing, and developing new thoughts, which, as he says :

> " . . . began to multiply
> Like sparks that from the coals of fire do fly."

His manifold experiences furnished him with rich and varied material for the characterisation both of pilgrims and pilgrim-opposers.

It is not necessary to set down directly to Bunyan's account the errors in orthography and punctuation which marked the first edition ; they are such as might easily have occurred in a small printing establishment of that day, with a compositor setting-up from a difficult manuscript—such as we may readily allow Bunyan's to have been, judging from the still-existing samples of his writing. It seems unlikely that he saw a proof ; but the mistakes were soon rectified. As to appearance, the book was small and insignificant, printed on yellowish-grey paper. It contained 232 pages ; the price was 1s. 6d.

Yet the popular verdict pronounced the production a masterpiece. The triumph was achieved almost entirely apart from the circles of the well-to-do, but it was great indeed. The sale reached the vast total of a hundred thousand copies even in the lifetime of the author.

That the minister of a poor dissenting congregation had, while mewed up in a wretched dungeon, produced a book which appeared likely to become one of the conspicuous glories of English literature, was not easy of realisation by courtly gentlemen who loved the smooth lyrics of Waller and the Puritan-baiting rhymes of Butler; or by fine ladies who adored the graceful verse of Dorset. It was not that they were by any means poor judges of literature. But Bunyan and his book were not of their world. His work was not to be taken seriously, but rather as an ephemeral fancy of the vulgar. The proper place for such quaint scribblings was among ignorant boors and in cheap-jacks' packs. That distinction in letters should be attained by a praying kettle-mender, who moreover eschewed the fulsome dedicatory flatteries by which half-starved pamphleteers made sure of patrons' guineas, and to which famous writers descended as a matter of course, was perhaps sufficient to brand even the *Pilgrim's Progress* as the production of an obnoxious crank, in the view of a gentleman of breeding.

It is well to remember that of the fathers of the language, Chaucer was of the Court; Wickliffe, albeit gloriously independent, a friend of John of Gaunt and a champion of Edward III against the Pope; and "the moral Gower," if we may elevate him into such company, in favour with Richard II; and if the lonely figure of Langland seems shadowily to stand aloof, at least we note that Piers the Plowman looks wretchedly poverty-stricken.

Again, the romantic literary figures of the Elizabethan day, like most of their forbears, found the Court their great magnet—the palace the place of attraction to all ambitious souls who fain would climb, whether politically, through serving the Queen; or socially, by flattering or amusing her; or in patriotic adventure, in seeking Eldorado or singeing the King of Spain's beard. The resort of all others, in which aspiring genius sought fame, not to say bread and beef, was the Court of Gloriana. Where patronage and ready money were, thither the struggling authors, conscious of ability and seeking a field of opportunity, gathered. But we cannot imagine the godly brasier as one of the glittering crowd. We cannot think of him between Ben Jonson and Shakespeare at the "Mermaid," or on bowing terms with Southampton.

This relationship of authorship to the monarch and the nobles was entirely natural, the social conditions, in the outworking and survival of feudalism, being what they were. Nevertheless, causes were at work which were bringing the author into direct touch with the people, and rendering literature less dependent on the patron. The revolution worked slowly but surely. The printing press had taken the place of the laborious scribe; Reformation principles were rousing the people to think. Puritanism and the Marprelate tracts and the Brownists were significant signs of the creation of new conditions. Then came the Civil War; and the Commonwealth.

The old ideas could never hold sway again to the same extent as in the old days. Yet, Milton was a classical scholar, and Latin Secretary to the Protector; and Andrew Marvell, although reduced to eking out his shoulder of mutton for several days, moved after all in a very different sphere to a humble person like Bunyan, who, even in the days when he preached to leading London congregations, described himself still as "John Bunyan, brasier," and was regarded by the mass of the well-to-do as notorious rather than famous.

The literary works of Penn and Barclay, were at least those of men of considerable learning and social standing. Baxter missed Oxford only through following the counsels of a schoolmaster who advised private tuition. But Bunyan was reputed an Anabaptist, a person of no education; moreover a determined upholder of conventicles, and an organiser and pastor of separatist congregations, a disturber of quietude and the magistracy; yea, and one who stoutly maintained that spiritual regeneration, and not graduation at Oxford or Cambridge, was the primary qualification for the Christian ministry. And as though these offences were not sufficiently rank, and did not constitute adequate reason for scorning him as a writer, he was—a tinker.

Kettle-bottoms and literary classics! Gravy-pans and words imperishable while the language should last! New-soldered roasting-jacks and visions of heavenly glory! Such associations of ideas were too preposterously grotesque for the superfine; and were calculated to provide rich food for cynics in an age that was first of all cynical. The idea of a pilgrim of the cross had small attraction for the frivolous mob that haunted the theatres of Portugal Street or Drury Lane, in the train of Charles, or dangled at the door of Barbara Palmer. The Elstow enthusiast might have furnished Etherege with the subject for a farce, or Wycherley with a foil in fustian for the giggling impudence of Nell Gwynne. When therefore the man of God broke in upon the gross darkness, with a sweet, simple, lovely picture in words of the sufferings and dangers, joys and triumphs, of a pilgrim of Jesus Christ, educated circles, traditionally and naturally associated with Courts and universities and theatres, paid on the whole but scant heed.

Yet, although the nation as a whole was

sunken in a slough of ungodliness far worse than that of Despond; although Epicureanism and calculating selfishness and sardonic contempt for honesty were the reigning forces, there remained a remnant of grace, whether in the old parish churches or the new meeting houses; and this godly remnant found in John Bunyan's prison book a delightful store of the honey of that Kingdom which is not of this world. And the great mass of ordinary folk, even if not themselves definitely of the pilgrim order, found it at once simple and entrancing; moreover an excellent book for the young people.

The *Pilgrim's Progress* made the doctrine and purpose of Christianity plain and familiar to great numbers of people who had never possessed a Bible, and never thought or meant to possess one; and in this sense the book, apart from its messages for the children of God, was a great evangelistic force. It was a book for the common people, when books for the common people were exceedingly few. The association with the trade of tinkering might be a drawback in the seats of the mighty, but it was none in the homes of the people. The characters talked in no stilted tongue, but in plain, neighbourly terms. The interest ran sparklingly to a noble conclusion, like a line of cohering quicksilver; the dialogue was sweet and wholesome as the scent of an old-fashioned English flower-garden; withal, the meaning shone with heavenly truth.

In other days, it became the custom to overlay the text with notes. These were admirably intended, and in some instances proved quite useful, but on the whole the plan tended to delay and distract; the pilgrims were kept "marking time" while enthusiastic commentators expressed sentiments of appreciation or explained the obvious. The effect was marred; the sun of Bunyan's native genius was obscured by innumerable cloudlets of annotation and sermonette. The practice has fallen unlamentedly into disuse: modern editions are of the Bunyan text, pure and simple. On the other hand, a highly valuable literature of Bunyan exposition has been created, drawing yet more honey from the Bedford hive, in a developed study of Bunyan characters.

When the Nineteenth Century turned its enquiring searchlights upon the *Pilgrim's Progress*, objections of an acidly critical character multiplied. The argument was urged that the repulse of Ignorance from the very gate of heaven was unfair. The point was that Ignorance should not, in justice, be blamed for not possessing knowledge, and that since he was at the trouble to make the journey, and ask admittance, he should have been allowed to enter.

The criticism however is ill-founded. Ignorance is not a pitiful, uninformed person, suddenly sentenced for not walking in a way of which he had never heard; he scorned wise direction, and made choice of "the religion of his own country"; which was "the country of Conceit." He is a type of the self-confident formalist, who, instead of humbly relying on Sacrificial Atonement, rebelliously flaunts his own merits: "I have been a good liver; I pay every man his own; I pray, fast, pay tithes, and give alms." He has not come in by the Wicket-gate, but through a crooked lane, and he insists: "As for the gate that you talk of, all the world knows that that is a great way off of our country. I cannot think that any man in all our parts doth so much as know the way to it, nor need they matter whether they do or no, since we have, as you see, a fine pleasant green lane, that comes down from our country."

Never really a pilgrim, but rather a blind, self-confident adventurer, he rejects saving faith. Vain-hope, the ferryman, helps him over the river; he comes with a swagger to the very door of heaven; only when he is asked for his certificate is he ultimately silenced. Ignorance has no word wherewith to answer the guardians of the gate; nor can the new Agnosticism furnish him with one.

Another objection ventured by academic unbelief is that "it would now be thought selfish in Christian to leave his kindred behind in the City of Destruction." But this is to confuse spiritual things with physical. Actually, the pilgrim remains among his kindred, usually, too, to their material benefit; it is his soul that aspires to pilgrimage; by the new spirit which is given him he walks no more in the ways of the world. The theory that an unconverted man is to persist in doing evil and being evil, until his wife and family can be brought to go on pilgrimage with him, will scarcely bear the examination of reason. There can be no true unselfishness in a weak agreement to refuse the higher call. And it is entirely appropriate for the head of the family to point the way out from the City of Destruction, and first of all to walk in it himself. Otherwise, Graceless never becomes Christian, and there is neither pilgrim nor progress. Moreover Bunyan has the pilgrim weeping and praying over his family; and that, too, with such desirable effect, that, although they at first deride him, yet, as Mr. Sagacity explains: "Second thoughts wrought wonderfully with them, so they have packed up and gone."

Criticism, indeed, has made but a poor display when challenging the tinker upon questions of faith and doctrine and spiritual consistency. Whitefield well said of Bunyan that he was "through grace chosen, called, and afterwards formed by the Holy Ghost to be a scribe ready instructed to the Kingdom of God."

Neither neglect by the superfine, nor sifting by criticism, has rendered the book one whit less attractive to the people. It was at once a bright mirror of the Gospel and of the daily experience of the humble Christian. Not only was its story arresting, but its message was powerful and vital. It was the greatest tract ever written. Trembling sinners saw their own mournful state reflected in the repentant man who feared that the burden he bore would sink him lower than the grave; and they forthwith resolved, like him, to go on pilgrimage. And the saints of God, harried by constable and informer and magistrate, were mightily refreshed by reading of such arduous conflicts as they themselves had fought in, of such communion with God and such deliverances by Emmanuel as they had themselves experienced.

To remark that Christian " stood typically " for the pilgrims and warriors of faith was but a cold saying, for the generation in which the book was published. For no hunted believer, recalling the brutalities of cabinets and judges, and the Scottish plunderings and outrages of Lauderdale, and " Danby and No Toleration," and more particularly, after all, the stern warfare of the soul, in which prayer had brought heavenly reinforcements for the conquering of heart-sins, could read without tears of the pilgrim, faint yet pursuing, fighting with dreadful Apollyon, withstanding the lurings of Vanity Fair, unlocking the dungeon of Doubting Castle, stopping his ears against whispering demons, and after climbing the table-lands of Beulah, descending to the margin of the deep waters of the River of Death, and being welcomed over by the shining host into the City of Light.

Thus, in the matter even of popularity, secular authorship was beaten, in open competition, by a simple allegory of the Christian life. Much as the " Doric delicacy " of *Comus* startled and delighted Sir Henry Wootton, so did the *Pilgrim's Progress* delight the poorer classes of England ; nor was the pleasure lessened by the knowledge that the author was not one of the earth's great ones, but was a plain Bedfordshire preacher, to whom rustics listened in meadows secluded from spies, or in the woods by midnight. In this prose poem, the godly noted how the brasier, whom the world of fashion looked upon as an " uncouth swain,"

"Touched the tender stops of various quills,"

in spiritual melody, and sang of the grace of God which bringeth salvation.

No small part of its acceptance with the crowd was due to the humour and aptness with which the characters were named. The men and women of the *Pilgrim's Progress* were not the dull abstractions of political dissertations or pasteboard Sir Foplings and Bellamours and Dorimants, but the very intimates and familiars of daily life ; and their names fitted them at least as well as their clothes.

All men might recognise strutting along the High Street—of Bedford itself or of any other town—Mr. Hold-the-world, with his chin high in the air, off to make hay while the sun shone; Great-grace, the King's champion, before whom fled the three sturdy rogues, Faint-heart, Mistrust and Guilt, after their assault upon Little-faith, would be known to all who attended Meeting. Both the saints and the ale-bench gossips might chuckle over Talkative, the son of Saywell, of Prating Row, who, although "his house was as empty of religion as the white of an egg is of savour," volunteered so glibly to talk of "things heavenly or things earthly; things moral or things evangelical; things sacred or things profane; things past or things to come; things foreign or things at home." And there would be no difficulty in understanding the famous Two Points of the religion of Mr. By-ends, of Fair-speech: "First, we never strive against wind and tide. Second, we are always most zealous when Religion goes in his silver slippers; we love much to walk with him in the street, if the sun shines, and the people applaud him."

Numerous are the passages of the *Pilgrim's Progress* which, whether descriptive of Gospel mysteries or the failures of sleepy saints, of scramblings through the Slough or welcomes to the city that shone like the sun, have been the delight of particular readers. A thousand happy touches make the book vivid, and endear the author to our hearts. The book, as Dean Howson says, is "a living bond between the devout and even the undevout, of all classes of mankind."

Indeed every turn of the road we tread in the tinker's company brings us to some new and surprising pleasure. The story almost insensibly broadens to a sublime end. The final passage glows with light. In describing the "Heavenly Jerusalem," with "the innumerable company of angels, and the spirits of just men made perfect," the author so soars with his subject that many a humble pilgrim of faith, after reading of the entering-in of Christian and Hopeful, while "all the bells in the city rang again for joy," has echoed the words of the dreamer himself, at the shutting-to of the gates: "When I had seen, I wished myself among them."

The book has occasionally the characteristics and verisimilitude of a verbatim report in a modern newspaper. The trial of Faithful, in Vanity Fair, is almost a real account of an actual assize case, so amazingly was justice perverted by a political Bench. The tyrannical judge, the subservient jury, the legal processes by which harmless folk were thrust into jail—all are preserved for our curious inspection in the clear amber of Bunyan's prose. We inevitably recall Macaulay's comment: "The imaginary trial of Faithful, before a jury composed of personified vices, was just and merciful when compared with the real trial of Alice Lisle before that tribunal where all the vices sat in the person of Jeffries."

In his own experiences with Kelynge and Twisden and the rest, and in his wide knowledge of the sufferings inflicted on so many who were his friends, Bunyan possessed ample material for a description of a typical trial scene. To realise its truth and force, we need only to refer to the trial of Baxter, before Jeffries. This indeed occurred some years after the publication of the *Pilgrim's Progress;* but if Jeffries had in the meantime studied the book by way of preparing a demonstration, for posterity, of the truthfulness of Bunyan's picture of a State trial, he could scarcely have presented a more vigorous and full-blooded Lord Hategood.

An account of the Baxter trial, given by an eye-witness, shows that Jeffries was in a characteristic spirit. True, when he mimicked the Puritan preachers, " squeaking through the nose," he received a quiet thrust from Pollexfen, the leading counsel on Baxter's side, in the adroit suggestion : " My lord, it is hard measure to stop these men's mouths, and yet not let them speak through their noses ! "

But this was only irritating the tiger. After flaming out at Pollexfen, the judge, with a rich vocabulary of vituperation, called Baxter " an old rogue, an old schismatical knave, a hypocritical villain " ; and when it was urged that "King Charles would have rewarded Mr. Baxter's loyal and peaceable spirit with a bishopric, had he but conformed," Jeffries, while admitting the fact, waxed more furious still, hurling such epithets as "conceited, stubborn, fanatical dog," and "snivelling Presbyterian," and declaring that the prisoner deserved to be whipped through the city.

In such brutal fashion the burlesque of justice was carried on, until Baxter mildly asked: "Does your lordship think any jury will pretend to pass a verdict upon me, upon such a trial?" The reply was: "I'll warrant you, Mr. Baxter; don't trouble yourself about that." This high degree of confidence, doubtless grounded upon the knowledge that the sheriff's officer would choose only reliable party men, was fully justified. Baxter was found guilty. The charge was one of publishing a seditious book. The trial was in any case a scandal. The sentence was a considerable fine; the prisoner was to remain in jail until it was paid, and was also to be bound over for seven years.

In justice or pity the candid admission may be made that jurymen in that day had much to fear. For example, for ignoring the orders of the Bench, in refusing to find William Penn guilty of preaching to "an unlawful, seditious, and riotous assembly" of quiet and peaceable Quakers, the members of a jury were fined, and sent to Newgate; and the Recorder of

London made the suggestive comment: " It will never be well with us till something like the Spanish Inquisition be established in England."

The trial in Vanity Fair may therefore be taken as a fair illustration of a case tried by such a judge as Jeffries, with such a jury as that of the Baxter trial. Bunyan himself was not tried by a jury, but his experiences of judges and magistrates were sufficiently varied. As to adverse witnesses, the character of the wretched informers who spied upon conventicles was common knowledge; Envy and Superstition and Pickthank would be quite well known in Bedford market.

With whatever realism Bunyan depicts the trial, he is yet clearly free from personal vindictiveness. The long imprisonment, the loss of home companionships, the sufferings of his family might have tempted him to retort upon his persecutors in their own spirit, but he drops no poison in the cup. True, he extenuates nothing; but he sets down naught in malice. The simplest record was, as we have seen, the severest condemnation; the torturing of humble saints in the name of the law was a process which carried its own condemnation. No great effort of the imagination is required to see in Lord Hategood's charge to the jury a reflection of the Clarendon Code; yet the spirit of pilgrimage does not allow the pilgrim to linger in the bitterness of controversy; he is to suffer rather than retaliate; above all he must needs press onward to the ultimate goal; he will presently come to the Delectable Mountains of Emmanuel's land.

Through the success of the book, the publisher, "Nathaniel Ponder, at the sign of the Peacock, in the Poultry," acquired the nickname of " Bunyan " Ponder. In the second and third editions the author made sundry felicitous additions; one of these introduced a new character, the famous Mr. Worldly Wiseman, who dwelt in the town of Carnal Policy and who directed the pilgrim to Mr. Legality (of the village of Morality), the very judicious man who had " skill to cure those that are somewhat crazed in their wits with their burdens."

The Second Part, relating, as we all know, the pilgrimage of Christiana and her children, and her young friend, Mercy, proved an admirable sequel. Some have seen in Christiana, the valiant Elizabeth Bunyan, who so splendidly fought her husband's battles with Twisden; and in Mercy, the young first wife, of whom we know so little beyond the fact that she spoke to her husband about her father's godly life, and that she contributed the two good books, the *Plain Man's Pathway to Heaven*, and the *Practice of Piety*, to the equipment of the humble home at Elstow.

If in vital interest the Second Part must be conceded to be a little less engrossing, and in incident a little less powerful than the First, yet it must be allowed to possess a peculiar charm. It realises the ideal of a Christian family, all of whom, with the widowed mother, are pilgrims. It brings us more pearls from the treasure-house of Bunyan's sanctified imagination. In spiritual beauty, some of its passages rival the finest in the First Part. But after all, although some comparison of the kind seems natural, it is really superfluous, in view of the fact that the two Parts make, not so much two entirely separate narratives, as two inter-related stories of pilgrimage which make a harmonious whole.

While noting the onward march of Bunyan's simple-hearted band, the mind turns almost instinctively to Chaucer and the Canterbury pilgrims. The resemblance, such as it is, is of course superficial; not of the heart of things. The well-fed and comfortably ambling company that sets out from the Tabard contrasts curiously with the homely and godly group of Bunyan's great allegory.

The style of both Chaucer's verse and Bunyan's prose is indeed breezily English; but as the Chaucerian troop make their way onward through Rochester and Ospringe and across Harbledown, we catch a whiff of incense from some, and of wine and spices from others, neither of which would have seemed grateful to Mr. Greatheart. And Christiana would have felt that she had missed her way had she found herself journeying as a fellow-pilgrim with the Wife of Bath. This is indeed to recognise Chaucer's fidelity and vivacious exactness. But it seems well to remind ourselves, in all simplicity, that while these two great " pilgrimages " of English literature are apparently somewhat similar, they are in reality essentially and totally different.

Touches of Bunyan's godly wit, shrewd character-drawing, and spiritual sensibility render the story of this pilgrimage of grace a delight. And that sweet lyric of the Christian life, the Shepherd Boy's Song, is like a spray of rosemary, whose scent carries a fragrant remembrance of the green and fruitful valley of Humiliation, which is beautified also with lilies, and where " labouring men have got good estates, for God resisteth the proud, but giveth more, more grace to the humble."

The climax of the pilgrims' Home-going is assuredly one of the most exquisite pieces of writing in all literature. When Boswell mentioned to Johnson, how Pope's voice had faltered during his reading aloud of the concluding lines of the *Dunciad*, the reply of the sage was: " And well it might, sir, for they are noble lines." Well may our eyes be dim as we read, even for the hundredth time, the lovely story of the crossing of the River by this pilgrim or that after the arrival of a summoning Letter of Love.

No picture of warfare ever presented such a scene of roll-call as this. Meissonier and

Butler are tame in comparison. For these ranks include not only conspicuous heroes like Mr. Valiant-for-truth, who crosses to the sounding of celestial trumpets; Mr. Standfast, who hopefully sends his prayers and tears to his wife and family, that peradventure they may follow in his way; and stalwart father Honest, whose last words are: "Grace reigns." Not only such noble figures of upward look as these, but likewise those in whom we behold a weakness which is almost pathetically grotesque, but which is Divinely endowed with transfiguring strength: Mr. Feeble-mind, who goes to the River saying: "Hold out, faith and patience"; Mr. Ready-to-halt, who bequeathes his crutches—all he has—to his son, saying: "Yonder are chariots and horses for me"; and Mr. Despondency, whose last words are: "Farewell, night; welcome, day"; with whom crosses his daughter, Much-afraid, who went through the River singing, "but none could understand what she said."

Christiana herself is however the first of the company to cross. The rest go with her to the River side. She leaves them with "a beckon of farewell." The last words she is heard to say are: "I come, Lord, to be with Thee, and bless Thee." So she enters in at the Gate. And, to quote the sweet and familiar conclusion of the story of her pilgrimage: "At her departure, her children wept. But Mr. Greatheart and Mr. Valiant played upon the well-tuned cymbal and harp for joy."

To relate the story of the book itself, in its ever widening circulation, is to recite simple facts which are "familiar in our mouths as household words." It might almost be said that to follow the history of Christianity during recent years is also to trace the progress of the Pilgrim in a new quest of soul-winning and spiritual instruction. When that mighty man of God, William Chalmers Burns, went out to Amoy, as the first missionary to China of the Presbyterian Church of England, he translated the *Pilgrim's Progress* as a means of evangelisation ; and when, a few years later, he penetrated into the interior, he rendered it into the local dialect. Similar stories might be told of many another whole-hearted missionary. The book has been translated into the tribal tongues of South Sea islanders, into Icelandic and Lettish, into Arabic and Hindustani, into Kafir and Yoruba, into Malagasy and Maori.

A vast literature has also grown up around it. Memoirs and character-studies of the author ; introductions and analyses ; metrical versions for children, in jingling rhyme ; variations and adaptions ; these multiply, generation after generation ; but while the innumerable majority prove to be only of ephemeral interest, the *Pilgrim's Progress* itself becomes more popular than ever.

The occasionally defective spelling and

other primitive roughnesses of the earlier editions have furnished ingenious editors with slight opportunities to smooth and rectify, but even in this matter Bunyan has not escaped ill-treatment. For example, in a conversation between Christian and Hopeful, the latter, speaking of the highway assault upon Little-faith, reminds his fellow pilgrim how Heman, although " a champion of his day," was similarly set upon. The reference is of course to the Eighty-eighth Psalm—which might well have been specially precious to Bunyan, so pathetically does it voice a " grievous complaint." The allusion itself implies that it had deeply impressed him ; and it suited his condition in jail : " Thou hast laid me in the lowest pit, in darkness, in the deeps . . . I am shut up and I cannot come forth." Nevertheless, the name of " Heman " being somewhat recondite, or the printer making a slight error, it became changed to " Haman." Subsequent wisdom revised the reviser. Southey, when preparing a new edition for a leading firm of London publishers, perceived the absurdity of representing Haman as being a godly sufferer, and seems to have turned for light, very naturally but quite mistakenly, to the Book of Esther ; in any case Haman's name was deleted in favour of that of his persecuted adversary, and " Heman," the Ezrahite, was thus transmuted into " Mordecai."

In the book's earlier days, piratical editions

and sectarian variations and continuations were not infrequent. Stimulated perhaps by Bunyan's hint, in the concluding words of the Second Part, that accounts of still more pilgrimages might be looked for from his pen, some unknown writer issued, five years after Bunyan's death, a so-called "Third Part." This feeble production, despite the fact that it was occasionally bound up with the genuine book, calls for no comment beyond that of John Newton, that "a common hedge-stake deserves as much to be compared with Aaron's rod, which yielded blossoms and almonds, as this poor performance to be intruded upon the world as the production of Bunyan."

While definitely entitled: *The Pilgrim's Progress—The Third Part,* no author's name was given; but the Preface was signed "J.B." Nathaniel Ponder denounced it, and at the same time announced the existence of a genuine but incompleted Third Part, by Bunyan, saying thereof: "The skeleton of his design and the main of his book, done by him as a Third Part, remains with Nath. Ponder; which, when convenient time serves shall be published." No such manuscript however has been published, and no other allusion to it has been traced.

On through the Eighteenth Century t' *Pilgrim's Progress,* while continuing to gr(in popularity among poorer folk, was s regarded by the educated classes gener;

as a mere cottagers' classic. Its strange destiny was, to work its way upward to the ranks of those who were reputed to be equipped to judge, from the ranks of those who were reputed not to be. " Bunyan's fame," said Southey," may be literally said to have risen ; beginning among the people, it made its way up to those who are called the public."

From the great writers of the Augustan age came no word of appreciation except from Swift, who declared : " I have been better entertained and more improved by a few pages of this work than by a long discourse on the will and intellect." Addison, while recognising Bunyan's popularity, did so regretfully ; but this may have arisen from a misconception ; it appears possible, since he classes Bunyan with Quarles, that he was founding his judgment, not upon the *Pilgrim's Progress*, but rather upon the little book of Bunyan's Gospel rhymes for boys and girls, entitled : *Divine Emblems*. Gay, in a skit in which Pope perhaps helped him, laughed at Bunyan, although " in a civil way," which showed that he regarded him as a spiritual force among the people.

Coming to the later part of the century, there is a sudden flash of recognition of Bunyan's genius. Boswell records that, dining one day at Topham Beauclerk's, Dr. Johnson, in the course of conversation, " praised Bunyan very highly." How the subject arose, Boswell does not say, but he quotes Johnson's critical judgment, that " his *Pilgrim's Progress* has great merit, both for invention, imagination, and the conduct of the story " ; and adds also the characteristic Johnsonian comments : " It has had the best evidence of its merit, the general and continued approbation of mankind. Few books, I believe, have had a more extensive sale. It is remarkable that it begins very much like the poem of Dante ; yet there was no translation of Dante when Bunyan wrote." *

When Johnson could thus speak of approbation being general, prejudice, it is evident, must have been growing gradually weaker, although history shows that it might appropriately have apologised, like Charles II, for " being such an unconscionable time in dying." And if Literature spoke in Johnson, Divinity found expression in Toplady, who had much in common with Bunyan, and who declared the *Pilgrim's Progress* to be " the finest allegorical work extant, a masterpiece of piety and genius."

* " As I walked through the wilderness of this world, I lighted on a certain place where there was a den, and laid me down in that place to sleep ; and as I slept, I dreamed a dream."—Opening words of the *Pilgrim's Progress*.

" In the midway of this our mortal life,
   I found me in a gloomy wood, astray
   Gone from the path direct. . . .
   How first I enter'd it I scarce can say,
   Such sleepy dulness in that instant weigh'd
   My senses down."
Opening lines of the *Divina Commedia* (Cary's Translation).

The next century saw a gradual increase of appreciation among the educated : the poor had never swerved from their love and admiration. Coleridge's view would doubtless carry special weight ; he said : "This wonderful work is one of the very few books which may be read repeatedly, and each time with a new and different pleasure. It is, in my conviction, incomparably the best *summa theologiæ evangelicæ* ever produced by a writer not miraculously inspired."

In spite even of such judgments as this, the feeling still lingered that Bunyan was an interloper in literature. It was as though some scarcely coherent "converted bricklayer" had intruded, in working dress, into the pulpit of Westminster Abbey, or some shabby scribbler of Catnach doggerel had enthroned himself in an erudite bishop's favourite corner at the Athenaeum. Cowper had recognised the position in the well-known apostrophe, which at once hails and conceals Bunyan under the title of "Ingenious Dreamer," and illuminatingly says :

> "I name thee not, lest so despised a name,
> Should move a sneer at thy deservèd fame,
> Yet e'en in transitory life's late day,
> That mingles all my brown with sober gray,
> Revere the man, whose Pilgrim marks the road,
> And guides the Progress of the soul to God."

That Cowper should write thus, even when such as Swift and Johnson and Toplady could be quoted on the other side, is good evidence of the persistence of prejudice. And Cowper had long moved in circles where he was familiar with the prevailing view of the upper classes, in the very district covered by Bunyan's more immediate labours in preaching.

This feeling of distaste was doubtless political as well as social. The strong love which some of the Nonconforming clergy felt for their old associations, and the reciprocal regard sustained by many who, like Tillotson, felt that their place was within the Establishment, but yet had no particle of sympathy with the old persecuting spirit of Laud, did not continue with any great fervency. And although peace-loving brethren on either side strove consistently for a better understanding, they were usually overborne by the force of controversy regarding disputatious points and strongly resented disabilities, by the warmth of opposing and firmly-held convictions which were fanned into a fire upon the hustings.

Bunyan, it was easy to recall, had used strong language on the subject of forced Conformity, and the cruel penalties contingent upon failure to attend the services of the Established Church. It was perhaps not always remembered with equal vividness that his long imprisonment was due simply to his insistence upon conducting services according to his conviction that he was thereby obeying in all simplicity the command of the Authority which he held to be supreme. He was looked upon with bitterness as almost a rebel, and altogether a sectarian. Yet the character of the *Pilgrim's Progress* shows that he rose above the accidental and the temporary to the essential and the abiding. The cherished thought of his inmost heart was, after all, of unity—" all one in Christ Jesus." His close friend, John Wilson, declared: " He was a true lover of all that love our Lord Jesus, and did often bewail the different and distinguishing appellations that are among the godly, saying that he did believe a time would come when they should all be buried."

An examination of his controversial works reveals the fact that it was invariably a spiritual principle for which he contended. The argument with Dr. Edward Fowler, vicar of Northill, Bedfordshire (afterwards vicar of St. Giles, Cripplegate, and then Bishop of Gloucester) furnishes an example. Fowler, who was the author of *An Apology for the Latitudinarians*, published a book entitled *The Design of Christianity*, which was intended as " A plain demonstration and improvement of this position, That the enduing men with inward real righteousness, or true holiness, was the ultimate end of our Saviour's coming into the world, and is the great intendment of the blessed Gospel."

Bunyan regarded the book as misleading

and indeed fundamentally unsound. Accordingly, he replied to it in : *A Defence of the Doctrine of Justification by Faith; shewing, true Gospel-Holiness flows from thence; or, Mr. Fowler's pretended "Design of Christianity" proved to do nothing more than to trample under foot the blood of the Son of God.* This is the little volume or good-sized pamphlet to which Macaulay referred in the famous sentence which states that Bunyan assailed Fowler "with a ferocity which nothing can justify, but which the birth and breeding of the honest tinker in some degree excuse."

Bunyan certainly used some strong denunciatory terms; and his general view of Fowler's book was not altogether shared by Baxter, who however thought it obscure and dealt with it in a pamphlet. A "reply" to Bunyan, probably inspired by Fowler, although not actually written by him, bespattered "the honest tinker" with epithets at least as bitter as any he had himself used; and, with a touch of local dislike, asserted that he was "infamous in Bedford for a pestilent schismatic." It was further suggested that the king would be rendering religion a service by inflicting suitable punishment upon the "impudent, malicious schismatic." There we might well leave the matter, but for Macaulay, for Fowler wins our regard, in another connection, by his courageous stand, giving a timely lead to the

o

London clergy, against James II, in refusing to read the Declaration of Indulgence from his pulpit at Cripplegate; and Bunyan commands our esteem by the zeal and skill with which he wrote in defence of Evangelical truth.

This vigorous treatise of Bunyan's must not be lightly passed by, as Macaulay's inadequate and complicating comment might be taken to imply, as a budget of vulgar and ignorant vilification. The personal allusions are only as bubbles on a mountain stream. The main body is an admirable exposition of the doctrine of Justification by Faith. It contends that the great fundamental of the Christian life is, primarily, faith in Christ Himself, and not simply an imitation of the character and virtues of Christ; before a man can truly follow, he must rest upon the Atoning Work. The argument, carefully and powerfully reasoned out, and founded upon Holy Scripture, is for a religion of spiritual regeneration and consecrated service in love, as against a religion of formalism and dead works of imitation. One passage says:

"Your description of a child of Abraham, you meaning it in a New Testament sense, is quite beside the truth. For albeit the sons of Abraham will live holy lives and become obedient to the substantial laws; yet it is not their subjection to morals, but faith in Jesus, that giveth them the denomination of children of Abraham—know ye therefore that they that are of faith, the same are the children of Abraham; yea, they that are of faith are blessed with faithful Abraham (Gal. iii. 7, 9)."

And further (again with regard to externals, this being of the substance of his exposition):

"You say 'that there is no one duty more affectionately recommended to us in the Gospel than is alms-giving.' Yes, that there is, and that which more immediately respecteth our justification with God, than ten thousand such commandments; and that is, faith in Christ. Alms-deeds is also a blessed command; yet but one of the second table, such as must flow from faith going before. . . . Christ Jesus did never set Himself forth for an example that we by imitating His morals should obtain justification with God from the curse of the Law; for this would be to overthrow and utterly abolish the work which Himself came into the world to accomplish, which was not to be our example that we, by treading in His steps might have remission of sins, but that through the faith of Him, through faith in His blood, we might be reconciled."

This will probably strike a dispassionate reader as being the language, not of a quarrelsome and savage sectarian, but of an ardent and sincere, if plain-spoken, champion of Gospel truth. In spite of the controversies in which Bunyan was from time to time engaged, it is clear that, while he was ever ready to combat for truth, one of his great hopes was that all who built on the Rock should be united in faith and hope and love.

The long neglect of Bunyan by the upper classes must not, however, be ascribed exclusively to social and political causes. One other reason, at least, there was, and it lay deeper; for it was spiritual antagonism that gave added force to the other prejudices.

In the decades immediately following Bunyan's death, spiritual religion was at an exceedingly low ebb. Ungodliness was not illustrated only by the familiar fact, told us by fiction, that "the British army swore terribly in Flanders." Society was honeycombed with unbelief. The first Hanoverian monarchs, too, continued in the immoral line of the last two male Stuarts. Speaking generally, and recognising that there were conspicuous stars amid the darkness, the Britain of Walpole and Bolingbroke, Townsend and Carteret, gradually sank into a terrible condition. Deism and Materialism prevailed. These were not the times in which to look for a new sense of appreciation of the *Pilgrim's Progress*.

When the Evangelical Revival broke out, under Wesley and Whitefield, it was admittedly greeted with a roar of hatred from the ungodly, both high and low; but nevertheless, through the days of darkness there had been sufficient of a Godly Remnant to call for edition after edition of the book, a fact which has a deep significance in view of the comparative scarcity of copies of the Bible among the poor. With the Revival there came a new and larger popularity, of which Whitefield himself spoke in a Preface to a fresh edition of the complete works, in 1767, when he said that " Mr. Bunyan's works, I hear, are enquired after and bought up more and more every day." The Revival strongly affected the educated classes as well as the poor. Chesterfield, although no one would venture the suggestion that he became a Christian, was at any rate greatly affected by the preaching of Whitefield, to hear whom the ladies of the aristocracy flocked to the Countess of Huntingdon's drawing-room.

The nineteenth century witnessed a still greater advance in general estimation. The extent of the change is evidenced in the announcements by which new editions were heralded. The book which in the old days had been peculiarly the delight of humble readers, and had been issued in a style commensurate to the meagre resources of the poor, was now the object of surprising care and even of reverence.

Eminent authors were called upon to contribute Biographical Prefaces. Distinguished artists were commissioned to supply the illustrations. And in the old-fashioned, cheap editions, which were still garnished with small wood-cuts—affording mingled joy and terror to generations of British children—the coat in the "Portrait of the Author" received the shining embellishment of a row of tiny gilt buttons, fixed on with adhesive.

Southey's reputation as poet and man of letters, and his position as poet laureate, enhanced the value of his new edition and new biography; and while we may regard his contribution to Bunyan literature as a singular mixture of sound view and warped judgment, although always expressed with sincerity and ability, it furnished evidence, in the very fact of its editorship and authorship, that the *Pilgrim's Progress* was at length attaining the position of universal esteem which its merits had all the time so richly deserved.

Argument regarding the permanent position of the *Pilgrim's Progress* in literature seemed to be ended when, as a "review" of Southey's edition, Macaulay's famous and beautiful tribute appeared, in December, 1850, in the *Edinburgh Review*. The political differences and administrative problems that had originated in the days of the Tudors and the Stuarts still survived—even as they do to our own day; and Macaulay obviously realised that he was dealing with a thorny and provocative subject, but he chose the wise and unifying plan, rather " to join in paying homage to the genius of a great man, than to engage in a controversy concerning Church Government and Toleration."

The essay is so familiar, that any comment upon it would seem an impertinence. Nor need it appear a sour and sweeping reference if we say that Macaulay's criticism of Southey, while undoubtedly sound, might, as regards several points of fact, be applied, in his own words, to himself; for, although "written in excellent English, and for the most part in an excellent spirit," it "propounds opinions from which we altogether dissent"; opinions that have by no means to do, as in Southey's case, with "excusing the odious persecution to which Bunyan was subjected," but which, as we think, place an under-estimating value on the reliability of Bunyan's confessions under conviction of sin.

It would however be contemptibly ungrateful to labour points of difference in face of the enormous service of Macaulay in vindicating the literary genius of Bunyan, and in further popularising his masterpiece; and it is a tribute to the power and fascination of the essay that after so many years have elapsed since it was written, no reference to it seems complete without quoting the noble tribute with which it closes:

"To our refined forefathers, we suppose, Lord Roscommon's Essay on Translated Verse, and the Duke of Buckingham's Essay on Poetry, appeared to be compositions infinitely superior to the allegory of the preaching tinker, We live in better times; and we are not afraid to say, that, though there were many clever men in England during the latter half of the Seventeenth Century, there were only two minds which possessed the imaginative faculty in a very eminent degree. One of those minds produced *Paradise Lost,* the other the *Pilgrim's Progress."*

The human interest that we all feel in Bunyan naturally extends to the people and the places that are most intimately associated with his life and labours. We are concerned to know what information can be found as to the valiant wife and the rest of the family. Not many particulars, however, can be ascertained. Elizabeth Bunyan outlived her husband by a year and a half. He had died a poor man, having apparently derived but little personal profit from the sale of his books, or at most only enough to meet ordinary household expenses.

Two children had been born to them—Sarah and Joseph; of the latter, scarcely anything is known; Sarah married a William Browne, of Bedford, and their descendants are still to be traced in the Midlands. Of the four elder children of the first wife, blind Mary died before her father; John, the eldest son, carried on the brasier's business, in Bedford, and (Dr. Brown tells us) was received into fellowship in the church of the barn.

Elizabeth married—in 1677, and therefore eleven years prior to her father's death—an esteemed member of the church, a well-to-do miller, Gilbert Ashley. Thomas seems just to have lived on quietly in Bedford—no details of his affairs are traceable, beyond a few entries referring to his family, which are found in the parish registers of St. Cuthbert's.

As to the places where Bunyan dwelt and toiled—since his birth-place, at Harrowden, and his cottage at Bedford have both been demolished, interest naturally centres chiefly in Elstow. Visitors from near and far make a pilgrimage thither, to look upon the pleasant village green where the sturdy young tinker played "cat," and stopped awestruck as the voice of God sounded in his soul; to peep into the ancient Moot Hall where he preached to people who all knew him well; and to linger awhile in the tiny garden of the cottage which was his home.

Time has dealt gently with the old places. Even the cottage remains much as it was in Bunyan's day, although the lean-to workshop has gone long since. The building is somewhat altered; when the crumbling plaster no longer kept the wind away, brickwork was substituted; and the exterior is now of rough-cast. Within, the flagstone floor has been removed in favour of red brick; but the wood-work abides. The great cross-beams and low ceilings still preserve an old-world aspect; and it is no difficult task to picture in the mind how the humble dwelling looked when it was the home of the inspired brasier.

Not far away, across the green, the bell tower still stands, and there the " alphabet " bell, which old tradition declares was the one rung by Bunyan, is still in its place ; and in the church the rough bench upon which he used to sit is still pointed out. And as we tread the village street we know full well that every one of those quaint old timbered houses and every green path breaking off across the fields was familiar to him.

In Bedford, the development of the town has swept away the buildings chiefly associated with Bunyan's memory. The county jail was taken down in 1807 ; and the narrow bridge over the Ouse, with its gatehouse-prison, has been superseded by a modern structure. St. John's Church, where Bunyan was a member ; and St. Paul's " steeple-house in Bedford town," where the Friends disputed with him ; as well as St. Cuthbert's Church, where his son Joseph was baptised, yet remain.

Our attention is now drawn mainly to Bunyan Meeting, which is to say, the cause which originated with " holy Mr. Gifford," and of which Bunyan himself was subsequently pastor. The present church building, which dates from 1850, occupies—like its predecessor of 1707—the site of the barn in which Bunyan preached on being released from prison, in 1672. A collection of simple but carefully treasured relics, in the custody of the Church trustees, includes Bunyan's chair, his little cabinet, and his water-jug. In the last century, the Church unhappily missed the opportunity of purchasing the house in St. Cuthbert's street in which Bunyan had lived during the latter years of his life; it was thereupon demolished; the site is now occupied by two tiny cottages.

While any personal mementoes of an excellent man and true servant of God have always their own peculiar and tender interest, we yet feel that to seek intimate reminders of Bunyan and what he was we turn almost instinctively to the places afield where he preached the Gospel at the risk of jail, and of separation from all that was humanly dear to him. We therefore seek out the quiet dells and woody amphitheatres wherein, to the accompaniment of the thrushes' songs or the whistling of the north wind, he broke the bread of life to the humble and harried poor.

To stand where thus he stood, and to go back in imagination through the years, and catch the sound of his voice in some Scriptural exposition or shrewd thrust or powerful appeal, is to be touched with a profound sense of reverence for his great-hearted valour and thorough-going faithfulness and patient endurance as a good soldier of Jesus Christ. But after all, in the nature of things such experiences are only for the few; nor, however delightful, are they essential. He speaks, he calls, from his own pages, and all may behold, shining therein, the true greatness and true humility of the Bedford prisoner who was so gloriously valiant for the truth.

No " pilëd stones " are required to remind us of him ; yet he is not without monuments. In Bedford, a statue has been erected, not many yards distant from the site of the jail where of old he made tagged laces for the support of his wife and family. In Westminster Abbey he is nationally remembered, amid the dust of monarchs and statesmen and warriors, in a stained-glass window ; while for Charles II no more memorial is deemed to be called for than the inscription of his name upon a small square of pavement over his grave. Sunlight gleams through the one, and shows the pilgrim ; but for a decent wooden barrier, men might tramp unawares over the other ; which things may be taken as parable, as well as fact.

But while the almost universal recognition of later times thus heaps honours on the dead, where the powers and dignitaries of the former day flung scorn and contumely at the living, the chief monument of John Bunyan is after all the love and admiration of innumerable readers, who follow, in eager thought, and haply with the kindling of spiritual aspiration, the onward march of the pilgrim company. Wherefore it may be, that when the stately memorials of stone and bronze and painted glass have passed to dust, it shall still be the happy custom, in the homes of those who love the Lord, to have one book in particular always lying conveniently at hand beside the family Bible, and that book,

THE PILGRIM'S PROGRESS.

THE END

THE CHRISTIAN LIBRARY

Classics of the Christian faith in deluxe, hardcover, gold stamped, gift editions. These beautifully crafted volumes are in matching burgundy leatherette bindings so you can purchase a complete set or pick and choose. All books are complete and unabridged and are printed in good readable print. **Only $7.95 each!**

ABIDE IN CHRIST, Andrew Murray
BEN-HUR: A TALE OF THE CHRIST, Lew Wallace
CHRISTIAN'S SECRET OF A HAPPY LIFE, Hannah Whitall Smith
CONFESSIONS OF ST. AUGUSTINE
DAILY LIGHT, Samuel Bagster
EACH NEW DAY, Corrie ten Boom
FOXE'S CHRISTIAN MARTYRS OF THE WORLD, John Foxe
GOD AT EVENTIDE, A.J. Russell
GOD CALLING, A.J. Russell
GOD OF ALL COMFORT, Hannah Whitall Smith
GOD'S SMUGGLER, Brother Andrew
HIDING PLACE, THE, Corrie ten Boom
HIND'S FEET ON HIGH PLACES, Hannah Hurnard
IMITATION OF CHRIST, THE, Thomas A. Kempis
IN HIS STEPS, Charles M. Sheldon
MERE CHRISTIANITY, C.S. Lewis
MY UTMOST FOR HIS HIGHEST, Oswald Chambers
PILGRIM'S PROGRESS, John Bunyan
POWER THROUGH PRAYER/PURPOSE IN PRAYER, E.M. Bounds
QUIET TALKS ON PRAYER, S.D. Gordon
SCREWTAPE LETTERS, C.S. Lewis
WHO'S WHO IN THE BIBLE, Frank S. Mead

Available wherever books are sold.
or order from:
Barbour and Company, Inc.
164 Mill Street Box 1219
Westwood, New Jersey 07675
If you order by mail add $2.00 to your order for shipping.
Prices subject to change without notice.

INSPIRATIONAL LIBRARY

Beautiful purse/pocket size editions of Christian Classics bound in flexible leatherette or genuine Bonded Leather. The Bonded Leather editions have gold edges and make beautiful gifts.

THE BIBLE PROMISE BOOK Over 1000 promises from God's Word arranged by topic. What does the Bible promise about matters like: Anger, Illness, Jealousy, Sex, Money, Old Age, et cetera, et cetera.
>   *Flexible Leatherette* .... $ 3.95
>   *Genuine Bonded Leather* $10.95

DAILY LIGHT One of the most popular daily devotionals with readings for both morning and evening. One page for each day of the year.
>   *Flexible Leatherette* .... $ 4.95
>   *Genuine Bonded Leather* $10.95

WISDOM FROM THE BIBLE Daily thoughts from the Proverbs which communicate truth about ourselves and the world around us. One page for each day in the year.
>   *Flexible Leatherette* .... $ 4.95
>   *Genuine Bonded Leather* $10.95

MY DAILY PRAYER JOURNAL Each page is dated and has a Scripture verse and ample room for you to record your thoughts, prayers and praises. One page for each day of the year.
>   *Flexible Leatherette* .... $ 4.95
>   *Genuine Bonded Leather* $10.95

Available wherever books are sold.

or order from:
Barbour and Company, Inc.
164 Mill Street Box 1219
Westwood, New Jersey 07675

If you order by mail add $1.00 to your order for shipping.
Prices subject to change without notice.